This book is due on the last date stamped below.
Failure to return books on the date due may result
in assessment of overdue fees.

FINES	.50 per day	

Key Concepts series

AGEING

Chris Phillipson

polity

First published in 2013 by Polity Press

Polity Press
65 Bridge Street
Cambridge CB2 1UR, UK

Polity Press
350 Main Street
Malden, MA 02148, USA

ISBN-13: 978-0-7456-3084-7
ISBN-13: 978-0-7456-3085-4(pb)

A catalogue record for this book is available from the British Library.

Typeset in 10.5 on 12 pt Sabon
by Toppan Best-set Premedia Limited
Printed and bound in Great Britain by the MPG Printgroup, UK

For further information on Polity, visit our website: www.politybooks.com

Contents

Acknowledgements

I owe many debts of gratitude for help in the preparation and writing of this book. Keele University – where I was a member of staff until November 2012 – was a major source of support in my development as a sociologist of ageing. I am extremely grateful both for the help and assistance provided by the University over the years and also to colleagues, in particular in the Centre for Social Gerontology. Many of the ideas and arguments were developed at conferences organized by the British Society of Gerontology and the Gerontological Society of America. I very much appreciated the critical comments and thoughts received at these events – they certainly assisted in the process of sharpening and clarifying the themes developed throughout the book. A large number of people in the community of researchers working in the field of ageing have also helped shape many of the arguments put forward. Jan Baars, Carroll Estes and Dale Dannefer have been especially important in furthering my understanding of theoretical issues in critical gerontology; they have also been inspiring friends and colleagues through the highs and lows of producing research. I am enormously grateful to them for their advice and encouragement over the years. I have also been helped by Tom Scharf and have greatly benefited from his work examining the causes of inequality and exclusion in old age.

I am grateful to the team at Polity, in particular Jonathan Skerrett, for consistent support and encouragement. The manuscript benefited from close reading by referees and from their friendly advice concerning ways of improving the text. Tony Warnes also provided a number of excellent suggestions about clarifying certain points in the manuscript, and I am in his debt.

This book would have been impossible without help and assistance from my wife Jane and our children Isabel and Luke. They have been a major source of inspiration and advice. Writing certainly invades family life, but in this case nothing would have been written without their constant encouragement. The book is dedicated to them.

Chris Phillipson

1
Introduction: Understanding Ageing

Ageing populations now exert a major influence on all aspects of social and economic life. Concerns about the best way of resourcing such populations, their impact on standards of living, and relations between age groups and generations feature prominently in public debate and discussion. The twenty-first century will without question be a time when all societies take stock of the long-term impact of demographic change and the implications for managing and organizing a major area of social and economic activity. Thus far, discussions have been tentative at best, discriminatory at worst, focusing on the apparent 'cost' and 'burden' associated with population change. Doubts about the value and purpose of ageing seem, if anything, to have become more not less strident in the present century.

The reasons behind the continued anxieties about ageing are at least fourfold. First, demography is of course important. Demographic projections (reviewed in Chapter 2) indicate that many societies across the globe can anticipate having up to one-third or more of their populations aged 60 and over by 2050. And the numbers are substantial – China, for example, is likely to reach a total of some 480 million people aged 60 and over by the middle of the twenty-first century. Second, the 'intensification' of ageing – resulting from continuing falls in fertility and continuing gains in longevity – has coincided with a crisis in confidence affecting institutions arising from the financial crash of 2008 and subsequent economic recession. Suddenly, population ageing – often viewed as a 'mixed blessing' by western governments – has assumed even more negative connotations. Demographic change could not be said to have 'caused' the economic crisis, but – it is argued – finding solutions will become ever more difficult given the rising tide of elderly people and the health and social problems which they bring (Liedtke and Schanz, 2012). Increasingly, governments fall upon the spectre of population ageing as a way of explaining why resolving economic problems will be difficult and why the pain incurred in searching for solutions will create challenges for all age groups. Third, the potency of fears about the consequences of an ageing population has been reinforced because these are no longer viewed simply through the lens of the nation-state. As will be argued throughout this book, the role of global organizations in interpreting population change has become of major significance. Global actors take concerns about ageing to a new and often dystopian level – linking it to other vulnerabilities which seem to beset what is presented as a 'runaway world' (Beck, 2000). Finally, ageing seems to be a problem because the moral framework which once gave it security (family and community in particular) is now seen as fractured and detached, seemingly cutting individuals adrift at a time when their need for help and support is increasing.

In responding to the above arguments, this book has set itself three main aims. First, it tries to make sense of the wider context influencing discussions about ageing, whether in terms of the characteristics of demographic change, trends in relation to work and retirement, the complexities of pension provision or issues affecting the provision of health and social care. The second aim is to undertake a critical inquiry about what is meant by terms such as 'age', 'old' or 'elderly people'. Indeed, one of the major points developed in this study is that misunderstandings about the nature of 'age', false assumptions about behaviours associated with particular 'ages', and the conflating of 'individual ageing' with 'population ageing' still influence many debates – lay as well as scientific. A third aim of the book is to provide a sense of the possibilities and potential inherent in ageing populations. Again, there is much work being undertaken in this area, to which reference will be made at appropriate points. But linking these discussions with a systematic overview of the nature and development of ageing populations, along with examination of the way in which ageing is socially constructed, provide a major focus of the present study.

Origins and arguments

This book builds upon my *Reconstructing Old Age*, published in 1998. That study pursued a particular argument: namely, that two key institutions supporting older people – mandatory retirement and the welfare state – appeared to be in decline, but with no obvious signs of replacement in respect of social and economic support. This book provides an opportunity to assess developments over the intervening period and to consider trends that might take place in the future. The changes affecting older people since the 1990s have been substantial. The institution of retirement has undergone further disintegration, with the policy of extending working lives now seemingly embedded in the discourse surrounding older workers. The welfare state has undergone similar transformation, with changes affecting a broad spectrum of activities from pensions to health and social care.

This study provides an opportunity to assess the implications of these developments. The argument put forward is that both sets of changes have created a sense of crisis for ageing populations. Mandatory retirement and the welfare state – for all their limitations (these are highlighted at different points of this book) – started to provide a framework around which ageing could be built. The uncertainty (to put the most neutral gloss possible on what have been seismic changes) affecting both institutions substantially deepened over the course of the 1990s and 2000s. Older people were enjoined to work even though the possibilities for employment appeared increasingly limited; they were tasked with creating their own sources of income over and above that provided by the state even while personal pensions declined in value; they were faced with organizing their own social care, under the guise of 'personalization', even though standards and quality of support were placed increasingly in doubt.

The above dilemmas and contradictions have been sharpened by two aspects which were less prominent when *Reconstructing Old Age* was written in the mid-1990s. First, although generational discord was highlighted in that book, it seems to have become a more prominent theme in UK and European debates since that time. True, there are prominent campaigns within the European Union and other bodies aimed at highlighting 'intergenerational solidarity'. But the entry of the 'baby boom' generation into their 60s has given rise to new predictions of generational conflict, notably over meeting the welfare entitlements of what is increasingly presented as an over-privileged group (Howker and Malik, 2010; Mandelbaum, 2010). Second, the terms of the debate appear even sharper than in the 1990s as a result of the anxieties arising from long-term changes affecting work and social life. The late Tony Judt (with Snyder, 2012: 385) captured this point when he argued:

> Gone is the sense that the skills with which you enter a profession or job would be the relevant skills for your working lifetime. Gone is the certainty that you could reasonably expect a comfortable retirement to follow from a successful working career. All these demographically, economically, statistically legitimate inferences from present to future – which characterised European life in the post-war decades – have been swept away.

The above quotation gets to the heart of worries about ageing – namely, that the institutions which might support this phase in life have been eroded to the point where insecurities and fears seem to have the upper hand. But the argument given in this book is that other possibilities also present themselves. 'Ageing' is viewed as a 'problem' because it seems to work against the grain of what is needed for a 'growing' and 'productive society'. Yet the reverse point can also be made: ageing and continued gains in longevity raise the possibility for renewing and re-engaging with activities and institutions that were abandoned in the period of dysfunctional economic expansion which characterized the 1980s through to the early 2000s (Tett, 2010). Ageing populations may not

restore balance to what is a chronic crisis affecting the economic system; but, as is argued in this book, they do
provide new ways of thinking about social life, offering in
the process radical solutions to supporting hard-pressed social
institutions.

On this last point, it is important to point out that the
arguments presented here are written from the standpoint of
a sociologist trying to think about ageing, using the tools of
social science, especially as applied to the field of social gerontology (the study of social aspects of ageing). The book
does not assume extensive knowledge of sociology, let alone
of gerontology. Rather, the aim has been to take the literature
within and outside these areas and see how they can illumi-
nate some of the issues and challenges raised by ageing populations. The sociological dimensions are also part of an
underlying argument about alternative ways of viewing
demographic change. The problem with conventional perspectives on ageing populations is precisely that they are
primarily looked at from a public accounting perspective. But
the concern here is to ask questions about how a group
known as 'older people' engages with and changes social
institutions (and vice versa). Crucially, the book puts to one
side certain assumptions about 'age' and looks instead at the
way these are built up through practices and activities which
arrive at particular definitions and conventions for treating
'old' or 'elderly' people.

Structure of the book

The book is divided into three main sections. Part I sets out
the context for understanding ageing populations, drawing
on demographic, sociological and historical approaches. Part
II extends the discussion by reviewing various examples of
changes affecting ageing populations, including pensions,
families and generations, and experiences in later life. Part III
examines proposals for change in a number of key areas,
including work, education and social relationships.

Part I starts off with a review of the development of population ageing, defining in the process what is meant by the

term 'ageing societies' (Chapter 2). The chapter contrasts population ageing across the global south and north and examines gender and social class variations in life expectancy, and the rise of what is termed the 'very elderly population' (including the increasing number of centenarians). The chapter also examines population change within a sociological context, exploring various influences on beliefs and attitudes about ageing.

Chapter 3 examines the ranges of theories developed to understand social aspects of ageing. The chapter considers the context for the emergence of social theory applied to ageing, focusing in particular on the expansion of sociology in the US in the 1940s and 1950s. The initial influence of functionalist theory applied to ageing is highlighted, as is the emphasis upon individual adjustment to transitions associated with retirement and widowhood. The chapter then considers the shift in theoretical perspectives from the 1970s and 1980s, with the development of theories of the life course and the application of approaches drawn from phenomenology, Marxism and feminism. The rise of critical gerontology is assessed, with an emphasis on the social construction of ageing and the link between social ageing and social inequality. The chapter goes on to review further developments in theoretical perspectives on ageing, notably those focused around the rise of the so-called 'third age' and the importance of consumption in shaping the lives of older people. The concluding section reviews the future of theory in the field of ageing, highlighting the importance of theoretical perspectives for understanding the challenges facing older people and the societies in which they live.

Chapters 4 and 5 explore a series of arguments and illustrations about the way in which 'age' as a social category is defined and constructed. Chapter 4 provides a historical overview of the way in which ideas about 'age' and 'ageing' developed, drawing together various changes from the early modern period to the twentieth century. These trace the emergence of old age as a distinct part of life, albeit one which carried different meanings according to gender and social class. Chapter 5 extends the discussion by highlighting the way in which retirement and the welfare state formed the framework through which ageing was built, underpinned by the idea of a life course constructed around education, work and retirement. However, the chapter goes on to demonstrate the 'destablization' of retirement in the twenty-first century and the emergence of new forms of risk and insecurity associated with growing old.

Part II explores some of the above themes with a more detailed review of particular areas. Chapter 6 develops a critical analysis of the field of pensions, highlighting the impact of neo-liberal policies which emerged in the period from the 1970s onwards. The chapter examines problems affecting the provision of pensions and assesses their more general influence on expectations and attitudes about ageing. Chapter 7 then looks at the role of family and intergenerational relationships in the construction of ageing, asking questions such as: Do families still form a major part of people's lives? Do generations work for or against each other? What are the implications of the changes accompanying globalization? In Chapter 8 we turn to what is referred to as 'late' old age and issues affecting people in their 80s and beyond. The chapter considers issues associated with the distinction between the 'third' and 'fourth' age, the impact of the 'bio-medicalization' of ageing and the crisis in the provision of care for people in institutions. The concluding section of the chapter explores the emergence of new fears and anxieties about ageing and how they link to the uncertainties surrounding the ending of life.

Part III of the book then considers some examples about how we might think in a different way about the potentials and possibilities of an ageing society. Chapter 9 sets out ideas for preparing for ageing populations, examining three main areas: new approaches to age integration, supporting older workers and lifelong learning. Chapter 10 continues the argument by identifying distinctive 'pathways' for later life, constructed through new forms of solidarity which can work across different generations and support a range of social groups and institutions. The areas identified are: mutual solidarities, family and friendship solidarities, caring solidarities and global solidarities.

This book was written at a time of intense debate about the costs and benefits of ageing populations. The entry of the baby boom generation into retirement contributed to soul searching about whether a 'selfish' generation was about to replace one that had been more 'deserving' of the benefits provided by the welfare state.[1] At the other end of the age spectrum numerous reports appeared to suggest a breakdown in the care received by people towards the end of their life.[2] More people started to write about their own ageing experiences or about caring for people with particular conditions associated with ageing.[3] And the thing that is called 'ageing' itself became elusive as people came to redefine later life in a variety of ways, challenging many of the conventional labels. This book is, then, about the concept of 'ageing': where it comes from, what it means and where it might it take us in the years ahead. In short, it asks: What do we understand by the concept of 'ageing'?

Part 1
Demographic and Social Dimensions of Ageing

2
Ageing Societies in a Global Perspective

Introduction

The twenty-first century has witnessed the emergence of population ageing as a global economic and social trend. Most countries in the world – even those with long-established older populations – are still in the process of adjusting to the implications of the changes involved. These are likely to be substantial, reaching into all aspects of cultural, economic and social life. Yet it is important to provide a balanced assessment of the type of challenges that demographic change will bring. Issues concerned with maintaining health and social care will doubtless occupy a prominent place in debates and will be discussed at different points in this book. But ageing populations will be transformative for society in various other ways, bringing innovative lifestyles, creating different types of communities and relationships, expanding the range of leisure and cultural activities and developing new institutions.

As will be argued, there are in fact many different paths likely to be followed by ageing populations. These will reflect factors such as social and cultural variations across different societies, contrasting levels of resources within and between countries, differences in the speed of demographic change and contrasting attitudes towards older people and the idea of ageing. The purpose of this chapter is to review the key demographic drivers behind population ageing, setting these within the broader global context which forms the organizational framework for this book. The chapter first reviews the development of population ageing, defining in the process what is meant by the term 'ageing societies'. It goes on to survey contrasts between different societies – both within high-income countries and in comparison with low-income countries of the global south. We will also consider gender and social class variations in life expectancy, and the rise of the very elderly population (including the increasing number of centenarians). The discussion then places population change within a sociological context, examining questions about the link between the development of ageing and individual beliefs and attitudes. Finally, the chapter considers a theme which will be returned to at various stages throughout the book: Why are ageing populations often presented as a 'problem'? What is the historical context for this? What alternative arguments might be developed in response to such views?

Population ageing in the twenty-first century

The ageing of populations was one of the most important developments of the twentieth century and will raise major challenges for life in the twenty-first. The proportion of the global population aged 65 and over in 1900 was 1 per cent (UK 5 per cent); in 2000 it was 7 per cent (UK 16 per cent) and by 2050 it is estimated that it will be 20 per cent, a figure that the UK is likely to reach in 2020. Population ageing refers to both the increase in the average (median) age of the population and the increase in the number and proportion of older people in the population. This change arises during the move from a demographic regime of high fertility and high mortality to one of low fertility and relatively low mortality. The former is associated with fast-growing young populations; the latter with more stable populations including a larger proportion of people in the older age groups. This process is described in the *demographic transition model*, derived from observations of the experiences of West

European countries over the course of the nineteenth and twentieth centuries. Two clear phases are identified in this model. In the first, mortality rates decrease as a result of economic growth, improved material well-being and advances in public health. Fertility rates stay high, however, leading to a rapid increase in the size of the population, reinforced by higher survival rates through childhood and beyond. Moving into the twentieth century, a second phase unfolds, with a decrease in the number of babies being born and greater prominence and awareness of older age groups (reflected, for example, in concerns about the danger arising from 'declining populations' expressed in the 1930s and 1940s).[1] By the second half of the twentieth century, in most European countries, birth and death rates converged to produce either stable populations or ones with relatively slow rates of growth (but with both influenced by the impact of migration).

Lloyd-Sherlock (2010) highlights limitations in the demographic transition model given its origins in western experiences of economic development, with trends in Asia, Africa and Latin American often at variance with those found in Europe. He notes:

> In a small number of countries with strong Islamic cultures or with extreme levels of poverty there is little sign of any significant or sustained drop in fertility . . . In many developing countries the 'lag period' between falls in mortality and falls in fertility lasted much longer than it did in Europe, greatly increasing population growth. In many of the same countries, the eventual fall in fertility was much faster than it had been in Europe. For example, in India the average number of children a woman could be expected to bear fell from 5.4 in 1970 to 2.7 in 2000. As a result, countries like India are now dealing with the consequences both of the long lag period (a very large total population) and of the halving of fertility in a single generation (rapid changes in its age structure). (Lloyd-Sherlock, 2010: 14)

Definitions of population ageing vary (see Victor, 2010 for a review), but a common approach in official surveys takes the relative size (percentage) of those aged 60 years and older (both sexes) or 60 (female) and 65 (male) and older within a given population. Gavrilov and Heuveline (2003, cited in

Victor, 2010: 64) suggest that, by convention, an ageing population is one defined as 8–10 per cent (or more) of the total population aged 60 years or older. Using this criterion, in 2007 there were 66 countries in the world that had 10 per cent or more of their populations aged 60 years and over, with a further 16 per cent in the 8–10 per cent banding (United Nations, 2009). On the other hand, Lloyd-Sherlock (2010) highlights the difficulties arising from using a particular age category (e.g. 60-plus), especially when drawing comparisons between richer and poorer countries. As his analysis shows, being 60 years old means very different things for women in countries such as Japan, India and Senegal, with wide variations in the number of years they may expect to survive and remain healthy.

In numerical terms, and with the above qualification in mind, the proportion of the world's population over the age of 60 is now increasing more rapidly than in any previous era. In 1950 there were around 200 million people over 60 throughout the world; this had increased to around 550 million by 2000. By 2025, their number is expected to reach 2 billion (United Nations, 2009). Globally, the population of older persons is growing at a rate of 2.6 per cent per year, considerably faster than the population as a whole, which is increasing at 1.2 per cent annually. The pace of demographic ageing is especially strong in the global south. Of the world's 65-plus population, 62 per cent (313 million) live in developing countries (2008 figures), where current aggregate growth rates of older populations are more than double that of developed countries (Kinsella and He, 2009). It is most noticeable in countries such as China, where fertility is well below replacement levels and life expectancy greater than 71 years. Projections suggest that by 2025 China alone will contain a larger number of older people than the population of the whole of Europe, with the proportion aged 65 and over doubling – from 6.9 per cent to 13.2 per cent – over the period 2000–25. In Asia, which contains the bulk of the world's population, median age[2] will increase from 26.1 to 38.7 between 2000 and 2050. Europe will age at a slower rate but from an older starting point, with the median age over the same period rising from 37.7 to 47.7 years. Oceania and North America will follow a similar pattern.

In absolute terms, the countries with the largest numbers of people aged 60 and over are China (160 million), India (89 million), the United States (56 million), Japan (38 million) and the Russian Federation (25 million). These countries account for around 45 per cent of those aged 60 and over worldwide, compared with European countries which account for 9 per cent (United Nations, 2009). By 2050, 32 countries are expected to have more than 10 million people aged 60 or over, including five countries with more than 50 million older people: China (440 million), India (316 million), the United States (111 million), Indonesia (72 million) and Brazil (64 million).

The demography of countries comprising sub-Saharan Africa (SSA) is more complex, given the continuation of high fertility alongside the impact of HIV/AIDS and the high rate of mortality among younger age groups. Two consequences follow: first, with rapid population growth, the absolute numbers of older people will increase; second, high mortality among younger people is likely to increase the proportion of older people in the population of many African countries. The number of people aged 65 and over is projected to increase by about 10 million in SSA between 1999 and 2015. While the overall population size will increase by 47 per cent during this period, the growth in the number of people of 65 years or older is set to rise by 57 per cent. Aboderin (2010: 412) notes that while sizeable proportions of older people in SSA countries are 'likely to be vulnerable to ill-health and poverty, this is not the case for all – or even most'. In this context, she makes the following point: 'We know little about the precise nature of social disparities in old age in SSA and about the life course and contemporaneous factors that give rise to them. This is compounded by the questionable merit of currently available measures for capturing older individuals' social and economic position or health status' (2010: 412).

International migration is another factor influencing the composition of ageing populations. The impact of migration flows from Asia and Africa to Europe (and similar south to north movements in the Americas) means that ethnic diversity will be an increasingly important factor in the make-up of older populations. The UK illustrates this point well: the

2001 Census showed just half a million people aged 65 and over from ethnic minorities. This number is projected to increase to 1.3 million by 2026 and 3.8 million by 2051, with especially strong representation by groups from South Asia. Reviewing these figures, Lievesley (2010) suggests that there is likely to be a sharp rise in the number of black and minority ethnic groups after 2021, with significant implications for policy and planning. This is because of the clustering of these populations in particular urban areas, the diversity of their needs in respect of health and social services, and the impact of lifelong inequality in shaping resources in older age (Nazroo, 2006).

The speed of demographic change is an important aspect influencing the capacity of national institutions to provide adequate resources and support. Population change in developed countries took place over a relatively long historical timeframe: France (where the outlines of an ageing population first emerged) took 115 years for the percentage of the population aged 65 and over to go from 7 to 14 per cent; in the case of Sweden it took 85 years; for Australia 73 years; and for the UK 45 years. The contrast for many developing countries is striking: China took 26 years; Sri Lanka 24 years; Brazil 21 years; and Columbia 19 years. The Chinese case illustrates very fast population ageing set to occur over the course of the twenty-first century. The proportion of persons aged 65-plus stood at 6.9 per cent in 2000. However, Yi and George (2010) note that under medium fertility and mortality assumptions, Chinese aged 65 and older will account for about 16.4 and 23.9 per cent of the total population by 2030 and 2050, respectively. Yi and George (2010: 425) highlight particular pressures facing older people in rural areas in China, a consequence of the massive migration of rural young adults to the cities and the limited availability of pensions (an issue repeated – given rapid urbanization – across many countries of the global south). With a projected total population of approaching half a billion older people likely to be reached in China by 2050 (representing one-third of the population), providing greater security and support will become an urgent issue for social and economic policy in the intervening decades (Yi and George, 2010).[3]

**Table 2.1   Percentage of population aged 65 and over.
Selected European countries**

Country	1985	2010	2035
Sweden	17	18	23
United Kingdom	15	17	23
Germany	14	21	31
Belgium	14	17	24
France	13	17	25
Italy	13	20	28
Netherlands	12	15	26
Finland	12	17	26
Spain	12	17	25
Ireland	11	11	19

Source: Office for National Statistics, 2012a

Ageing in europe and the rise of the 'oldest old'

The demographic transition from high to low mortality and fertility occurred first in Europe, and the region remains a 'global leader' in respect of the population aged 65 and over (Kinsella and He, 2009; see also Table 2:1). The demography of Europe, however, shows considerable variation (Office for National Statistics [ONS], 2012a). Within the EU-27, Germany and Italy – both with consistently low fertility – are the countries with the highest proportions aged 65 and over (21 and 20 per cent respectively); Slovakia, Cyprus and Ireland are the least aged, with 13, 12 and 11 per cent of their populations aged 65 and over respectively. By 2035, 23 per cent of the UK's population is projected to be 65 and over, although this is at the low end of the European continuum – substantially so in comparison with Germany (at 31 per cent) and Italy (28 per cent). Beyond Europe, Canada, Australia, New Zealand and the United States have smaller proportions of older people than many of the EU-27 countries. In 2010, 14 per cent of the populations of both Canada and Australia were aged 65 and over, compared with 13 per cent in New Zealand and the United States.

The constituent countries of the UK have experienced both population ageing and the progressive ageing of the older population – i.e., more people surviving into their 80s, 90s and beyond. On the first aspect, the percentage of the population aged 65 and over increased in England and Wales from 15.9 per cent in 2001 to 16.4 per cent in 2011, an increase of nearly 900,000 people (ONS, 2012b). By comparison, over the same period, the percentage of the population aged 0–14 decreased from 20.5 per cent in 1985 to 17.6 per cent in 2011. There is some variation across the constituent countries of the UK, illustrated in particular by Wales, where the combination of out-migration of young people and in-migration of retirees leads to a projection of 26 per cent of the total population 65-plus by 2035 (compared with 18.4 per cent in 2011).

The second dimension concerns the ageing of the older population, reflected in the growth in the numbers of people aged 80 or 85 and over. The UK has seen a doubling in the population aged 85 and over in the 25 years from 1985: from 690,000 to 1.4 million people, with a projected increase to 3.6 million (5 per cent of the total population) by 2035 (ONS, 2011a). While the UK population grew by 4.2 per cent between 2002 and 2009, the numbers of people aged 85 and over grew by 21.5 per cent (ONS, 2011a). On a global level, the 80-plus population is projected to increase by 233 per cent between 2008 and 2040, compared with 160 per cent for those aged 65 and over and 33 per cent for the total population of all ages. Japan represents the extreme end of the continuum: by 2040, 38 per cent of all older Japanese are expected to be at least 80 years old, up from 26 per cent in 2008 (Kinsella and He, 2009: 28). Alongside this has come the rise of centenarians (most of whom are female) as a distinct group within the older population (Serra et al., 2011). In the UK in 2011, the probability of an individual aged 80 living to 100 was 6.2 per cent for men and 9.2 per cent for women. UK estimates for the size of the group aged 100-plus was 12,640 in 2010, with projections suggesting a rise to least half a million by 2066 (Department for Work and Pensions, 2011a). At a global level, the population of centenarians was estimated at around 270,000 in 2005, with a projected increase to 2.3 million by 2040 (United Nations, 2009: cited in Kinsella and He, 2009).

Such increases raise considerable implications for the adequacy of pensions and the quality of health and social care services (as will be explored in Chapters 6 and 8), with particular challenges for both low-income countries (where more than half of the oldest-old can be found) and those on low incomes in the richer countries of the world. Indeed, the failure to provide adequate resources for those at the end of their life remains a major cause of concern. The so-called 'oldest-old' (those aged 85 and over) are, as a group, at greater risk of poverty than younger older people (aged 65–84) (Hills et al., 2010). Serra et al. (2011: 7) make the point that 'poverty (as measured by income) among centenarians may be more amplified than among the oldest old group (85–89) given their longer spells of economic inactivity'. Women are especially vulnerable here, given the typical work histories of this cohort (and almost certainly succeeding cohorts) of low-income and limited pensions. Other sources of vulnerability for those aged 85 and over include severe limitations in activity (experienced by 55 per cent); high levels of depressive symptoms of clinical relevance (23 per cent); and the likelihood of a substantial decrease over time in the quality of life.[4] Given the substantial rise in those 85 and over by 2035, designing effective income and welfare policies for this age group will become increasingly urgent, and an issue to which we shall return later in this book.

Extended lives: Demographic and social contrasts

A key dimension to ageing populations, as already noted, is the combination of low fertility on the one side and long lives on the other. The extension of life – amounting to some 30 years in Western Europe over the course of the twentieth century – can certainly be viewed as a major achievement for public health and state intervention in welfare. The figures are indeed striking. Christensen et al. (2009: 1196) calculate that if the pace of improvements in life expectancy continues through the twenty-first century, 'most babies born since 2000 in France, Germany, Italy, the UK, the USA, Canada, Japan, and other countries with long life expectancies will celebrate their 100th birthdays'. They go on to note that data from more than 30 developed countries 'showed that in 1950 the probability of survival from age 80 years to 90 years was on average 15–16 per cent for women and 12 per cent for men. In 2002, these values were 37 per cent and 25 per cent' (Christensen et al., 2009: 1197). The case of Japan, where the probability of surviving from age 80 years to 90 years now exceeds 50 per cent for women, illustrates the scale of the change.

Gender differences in life expectancy remain important, though the rate of change for *both* men and women is again striking. In 1981, men in the UK at age 65 could expect to live a further 14 years; by 2008–10 the figure had increased to 17.8 years; by 2051 it is expected to be 25.9 years. The equivalent figures for women – which show the gender gap maintained, albeit narrowed – are, respectively, 18 years, 20.4 years and 28.3 years (ONS, 2011a; 2012a; 2012b). These figures are repeated across most high-income countries, though with significant differences when comparing different socioeconomic groups and neighbourhoods (see further below). For low-income countries of the global south, life expectancies are lower and the gender gap in life expectancy is much smaller. For example, life expectancy at birth in Botswana is 41.7 years for men and 41.3 years for women; in Somalia it is 45.1 years for both sexes. For many SSA countries, along with the transitional economies of the former Soviet Republic, life expectancy was at a lower level by the first decade of the 2000s as compared with 1990, reflecting the influence of factors such as market-orientated economic policies, the impact of HIV/AIDS and poor-quality healthcare.[5]

Making appropriate adjustments to the key demographic change (that very few people – especially in Western Europe – die young) to social structures and attitudes is more complex. There is, first of all, the historical weight of institutional and cultural practices towards older people. In tracing attitudes towards ageing from antiquity to the renaissance, Minois

(1989: 303) concluded: 'In spite of the various pleas in defence which we have met, it is clear that youth has always and everywhere been preferred to old age. Since the dawn of history, old people have regretted their youth and young people have feared the onset of old age.' Peter Stearns (1977: 42), commenting on the experiences of working-class people in the eighteenth and nineteenth centuries, argued:

> Workers expected to grow old early, by modern standards; what was middle age even to other contemporaries was old age to them. But more basically the concept of aging was itself foreign; one lived, deteriorated a bit, and died. The notion of a distinct period of life – quite apart from the problem of whether this began at fifty or sixty-five – was lacking.

To be sure, many tracts were written identifying ways of prolonging life and avoiding premature death – Luigi Cornaro's (1557) *Discorsi della vita sobria* [*A Treatise of Health and Long Life with the Sure Means of Attaining it*] being an oft cited-example. But these tended to have limited influence or appeal to a mass audience, given the realities and hardships associated with old age (Achenbaum, 2010).

Twenty-first-century experiences of life expectancy illustrate continuities with previous historical periods. Stearns (1977: 42) makes the point that: 'In modern society one of the main functions of social class has been to prepare a differential response to aging, just as in earlier times social stratification served significantly to differentiate the trappings of death.' As will be argued at different points of this book, working-class attitudes remain ambivalent about ageing, grounded in realities associated with differences in life expectancy as well as financial and social inequalities. The Marmot Review *Fair Society, Healthy Lives* (Marmot et al., 2010) found that although life expectancy increased for everyone between 1971 and 2005, the gap in life expectancy by social class for men and women had persisted, with some widening taking place over the period of the 1980s and 1990s. These were carried through in the following decade, with statistics in the UK showing that although life expectancy increased for all social classes, improvements were more rapid for those in 'higher managerial and professional' as opposed to 'routine' occupations. In 1982–6 men in the former group could expect to live 2.3 years longer at age 65 than the latter; by 2002–6, this gap had increased to 3.5 years, with the managerial/ professional group expected to live for 18.8 years and routine workers for 15.3 years. Women showed similar social class inequalities, although the gap between highest and lowest social classes did not increase over the same time period (ONS, 2012b)

Evidence from the Marmot Review (2010) for the 'social gradient of health' was especially striking, with people aged 45–64 in routine and semi-skilled jobs having rates of illness comparable to those 65 and over in the managerial and professional classes. And the contrasts in life expectancy between working-class and middle-/upper-class communities have been widely documented, with examples such as life expectancies for men aged 65 and over in the London Boroughs of Kensington and Chelsea and Westminster of 22.7 years and 21.2 years respectively compared with 13.9 years in Glasgow City and 15.5 years in Manchester and Liverpool. As the Marmot Review (2010: 37) observes: 'In the poorest neighbourhoods of England, life expectancy is 67, similar to the national average in Egypt or Thailand, and lower than the average in Ecuador, China and Belize, all countries that have a lower GDP and do not have an NHS.'

The achievement of more people living into their 80s and beyond is of course a real one. But the gap between the man in Kensington and Chelsea with a life expectancy of 88 years and the man in Tottenham Green with one of 71 years is also real. At the same time, the question of whether people are 'prepared' for, or even 'believe' in, the possibility of an extended life remains uncertain. Researchers such as Peter Laslett (1989) and Gilleard and Higgs (2005) have argued the case for a 'third age', where people have the freedom to take control of their lives ahead of the period of decline associated with the so-called 'fourth age' (see further Chapters 3 and 8). This third age is viewed as a 'cultural field' built around the lifestyles and interests associated with the first-wave baby boom generation – i.e., those born in the late 1940s and early 1950s. With this development, there appeared to be a match between twentieth-/twenty-first-century achievements in life expectancy and the emergence of a social and cultural space aimed at fulfilling the potential of growing old. Yet even here, as will be explored in more detail later in this book, class (along with gender and ethnic) differences remain of considerable importance. Chatzitheochari and Arber (2011) examined time use among older people and evidence for the pursuit of active lifestyles in the third age. The findings of their research pointed to the continuation of marked social divisions in third age lifestyles:

> [O]lder British people mostly participate in indoor leisure activities that could be characterized as 'low demand', such as watching television and other passive forms of media consumption. The active and self-fulfilling 'ideal' time period following retirement . . . is more likely to eventuate for healthy men of a privileged educational and occupational background.

They conclude: '[S]ystems of gender and class inequality and disadvantage continue to operate after retirement, and . . . the cultivation of an active leisure lifestyle is inextricably intertwined with an older person's social characteristics and previous life-course experiences.'

Other factors also contribute to improvements in life expectancy and resistance to, or negative beliefs about, ageing. The difficulties which workers in the eighteenth and nineteenth centuries had of identifying with a 'distinct period' of life after 50 or 60 appeared to have been resolved with the institutionalization of retirement (beginning in the early twentieth century), supported by the founding of the welfare state (in the mid-twentieth century). These institutions seemed to provide a framework both for supporting growing numbers of older people and for securing legitimacy for ageing itself (Phillipson, 1998). But, as will be discussed elsewhere in this book, the vision underpinning retirement and the welfare state began to unravel in the 1970s, before finally imploding in the first decade of the twenty-first century. Such developments have brought to the surface profound tensions in the way ageing is viewed within society. Writing in the early-1990s, Thomas Cole (1992: 237) was expressing concern about the inability of western culture to 'provide convincing answers to . . . existential questions [such as] the quality of life in old age, the unity and integrity of the life cycle and the meaning of aging' (see also Baars, 2012). Two decades on it is clear that these questions remain unanswered but, at the same time, have themselves become sources of conflict given a social context of economic crisis and generational tensions. Clarifying some of the issues involved and the changing meaning of ageing with which they are associated will be a key concern of the various chapters of this book.

Conclusion: Is population ageing a 'problem'?

The development of ageing populations has always attracted a significant degree of controversy. This has been expressed in different ways, reflecting economic and political conditions prevailing at particular points in time (Phillipson, 1982). The existence of a certain proportion of people over a particular age has tended to create unease and insecurity within society. The dividing line taken has invariably been somewhat arbitrary – 55, 60, 62, 65, 70 – but whatever point is taken seems as likely to provoke negative rather than positive views about the probable impact on institutions and resources (Mullan, 2000). In the 1940s, when Britain faced a declining birth rate, Richard and Kay Titmuss (1942) warned: 'We are up against something fundamental, something vast and almost terrifying in its grim relentless development.' They expressed concern that an ageing society would 'lose the mental attitude that is essential for social progress . . . the future . . . will require greater intelligence, courage, power of initiative, and qualities of creative imagination . . . qualities . . . not usually to be found in the aged' (cited in Blaikie, 2006: 13).

In the 1970s and 1980s, the financial consequences of population ageing came under scrutiny, notably in relation to the size and alleged 'burden' both of pension provision in particular and welfare states more generally (Longman, 1987; Johnson et al., 1989). Older people were depicted as a 'selfish welfare generation' (Thomson, 1989) or 'greedy geezers' (*New Republic*, 28 March 1988), diverting resources from the young while contributing to substantial public expenditure deficits. In the area of healthcare, the biomedical ethicist Daniel Callahan (1987) started a major debate in the US, following publication of his book *Setting Limits: Medical Goals in an Aging Society.* Callahan identified three aspirations for ageing societies: first, to stop pursuing medical goals that combine the features of high costs, marginal gains, and benefits (in the main) for the old; second, that older people should shift their priorities from their own welfare to that of younger generations; and third, that older people should accept death as a condition of life, at least for the sake of others. Callahan's intervention, unsurprisingly, attracted considerable debate and dissension (see, especially, Homer and Holstein, 1990) but it fuelled an already highly charged debate concerning the potentially contrasting interests of younger and older generations.

In the 1990s, the debate about ageing shifted from an exclusive focus on financial and public costs to a more generalized set of anxieties associated with living in what sociologists such as Giddens (1991) and Beck (1992) termed as the 'risk society'. Ageing populations were linked with other crises such as climate change and global terrorism, and viewed as developments likely to destabilize existing social and political institutions (Mullan, 2000). Thomas Cole (1992) argues that personal anxieties about growing old became conflated with pessimism for the future: 'Critics and commentators represent[ed] the aging of . . . social institutions with metaphors of decline, exhaustion and collapse.'

By the 2000s, both sets of concerns – ageing as an 'economic burden' and as a source of 'cultural anxiety' – were fused, notably around a new 'moral panic' in relation to the movement into late life of the post-war baby boom generation (Phillipson et al., 2008; Willetts, 2010; see further Chapter 5). The demographic context was the increase in the birth rate which took place across industrialized countries from the mid-1940s through to the mid-1960s. In reality, this phenomenon varied substantially from country to country – highly compressed in some (e.g. Finland), extended in others (e.g. Australia and the US) and, exceptionally, split between separate time periods in the case of the UK. The debate has tended to fuse these contrasting experiences, presenting a surge in the population entering retirement as having the potential to wreak economic havoc as well as damage the life chances of younger generations (Howker and Malik, 2010; Berry, 2012).

The concerns raised about population ageing will be discussed at different points in this book, in relation to issues such as how ageing and old age are defined and constructed; the relationship between social inequalities and ageing; issues relating to generations and ageing; and questions concerning economic and social resources. In developing these arguments, we might at this stage note the following points as a framework within which more detailed observations might be made. In the first place, and especially important from a sociological perspective, is the diversity contained within the groups classed as '*older people*' or '*ageing populations*'. The former covers a wide range of age and social groups and there is no obvious cut-off point separating 'earlier' from 'later' life. Of course, there are many important experiences which tend to cluster towards the latter end of life – not least widowhood, particular changes in social and economic statuses, and certain types of illnesses. But even here, variations are immense both in the range of conditions and the way they are experienced. And ageing populations themselves are subject to wide demographic variations, with societies ageing at different rates, with diverse characteristics, and with contrasting social and economic resources at their disposal. Lloyd-Sherlock (2004: 6) summarizes the dangers of generalizing about later life from either a negative or positive perspective:

> [S]ome older people have high levels of vulnerability and dependence, others may be making more social and economic contributions than at any previous time in their lives, and the great majority are both dependent and depended upon. The main shortcoming of these opposed viewpoints is that they portray later life as a common experience. A more balanced perspective requires an appreciation of later life as a fluid, complex and heterogeneous phenomenon.

Arising from this, a second observation examined throughout this book concerns the case for a different type of language to portray population ageing and relationships between generations. This approach would stress, following the above, the *interdependency* of age groups and generations facing radical changes to aspects of their social and economic position. We appear to be entering a new type of life course, one in which needs and abilities are no longer entirely subordinate to chronological boundaries and bureaucratic mechanisms (Cole, 1992). In the 1980s and 1990s, as already noted, the balance of debate swung toward expressions of doubts about the benefits of population ageing (Vincent, 2003). Despite the radical critique offered by those working in the area of critical gerontology (see Chapter 3) and the activities of groups of older people themselves, emphasis was placed on the contrasting needs and interests of different generations. For the twenty-first century, however, a process of renewal in generational politics is required. The basis for this will stem from recognition that presenting issues in terms of younger *versus* older generations will frustrate positive solutions to the needs of young *and* older people – in high- as well as low-income countries. As Heclo (1989: 387) observes:

> In an already fragmented society such a framework would be especially unconstructive. It would divert attention from disparities and unmet needs within age groups. It would help divide constituencies that often have a common stage. Above all, a politics of young versus old would reinforce an already strong tendency . . . to define social welfare in terms of a competitive struggle for scarce resources and to ignore shared needs occurring in everyone's life-cycle.

Recognition that we are constructing a different type of life course may also help form the basis for a new generational politics. Here, the worker versus pensioner perspective is especially unhelpful in that it ignores fundamental changes to the distribution of labour across the life course. The labels 'worker' and 'pensioner' are less easy to define when the stages that separate them are undergoing change. For many workers the predictability of continuous employment is being replaced by insecurity in middle and later life, as will be illustrated later in this book. The implication of the radical changes affecting the life course is that responsibilities for an ageing population cannot be 'offloaded' to particular generations or cohorts – whether old, young or middle-aged. Ageing is an issue *for* particular generations, but it is also a question to be solved *across* generations. The following chapters of this book set out different ways of approaching this issue as well as setting an agenda for change in preparing for an ageing society.

3
Social Theories of Ageing

Introduction

The purpose of this chapter is to review some of the main theories developed by sociologists and allied disciplines involved in studying social aspects of ageing. Theory makes an important contribution to insights about ageing, suggesting new hypotheses to test through empirical research. Bengtson et al. (2009: 4) view theory as playing the role of attempting to explain the various puzzles encountered in the process of undertaking research: 'Whether in the laboratory, in field studies, or in surveys – or indeed in everyday life – humans seek explanations and meanings for *what* they observe or experience. And that leads to their questioning the *why* and the *how* beyond their immediate observations. This is theorising – the search for explanation' (emphasis in original).

This search is important in all scientific undertakings but has particular resonance for the task of understanding ageing. Reference was made in the previous chapter – and will be developed further in Chapter 4 – to the complex way in which ideas about 'age', 'ageing' and 'old age' have evolved through different historical periods. We might also note misleading assumptions about ageing that are often left unquestioned – even among those involved in the study of later life. So using theory (or *theorizing* to use the more active terminology) both to question and explain is essential for taking forward understanding about the way in which ageing is constructed.

Social theory is especially important to the focus of this book in view of the argument – laid out in Chapter 2 – that ageing can only be understood within the context of social environments, with the two working together in complex ways that shape the individual's journey through the life course. This point has been elaborated by Dannefer (1999) in his review of approaches to understanding the relationship between the individual organism and the surrounding environment. The first he describes as the parallel or dichotomous approach whereby the organism is viewed as being born into a pre-given environment; its success is based on its capabilities to survive to reproduction in that environment. The second perspective focuses on how discrete organisms and discrete environments influence each other in a range of interactions:

> This approach can be called interactive or dialectical because it centres on the dynamics between an actual individual and the immediate environment. The individual is shaped to varying degrees by its exchanges with the environment, and these exchanges also affect the environment itself . . . In the parallel model, individual and environment are largely pre-structured entities that engage in a matching game (a game in which natural selection plays a central role); in the dialectical model, individual and environment are not fixed entities to be 'matched', but are continuously being reconstituted in everyday interaction. (Dannefer, 1999: 69)

The distinction made by Dannefer is helpful in thinking about the relationship between 'ageing' on the one side, and 'society' on the other. This book explores how ageing is constructed through social and cultural institutions which provide the basis of what it means to be 'young', 'middle-aged' or 'old' (Schaie and Achenbaum, 1993). Equally, grouping people within these classifications also changes society in significant ways – both its image of itself (as 'young' or 'old') and in the range and type of institutions which it develops (Featherstone and Wernick, 1995; Estes et al., 2003).

The aim of this chapter is to explore the ties between ageing and society and the different ways these have been understood through the application of social theory. A number of reviews are readily available on this topic – for example, those brought together in the volume of essays by Bengtson et al. (2009) and in chapters in books edited by Settersten and Angel (2011) and Binstock and George (2011). This chapter does not attempt to duplicate those contributions; rather, it uses them to explore the way in which social theory can be used to further our understanding of the various links between 'age' and 'social structure'. The first section of the chapter examines the context for the development of social theories of ageing, highlighting strengths as well as weaknesses in the way in which theory developed. The remaining sections examine particular theoretical approaches and their implications for understanding social processes associated with ageing.

Society and ageing: Context and theory

Social theory applied to ageing can be traced back to the 1940s and early 1950s, a period when western societies – still struggling with the economic and social consequences of the Second World War – were also adjusting to the implications of ageing populations. In the UK, research – at least up until the 1980s – was dominated by the view that ageing was a 'welfare' or 'social problem', with studies undertaken largely outside the discipline of sociology. This was less characteristic of the US, where the absence of a welfare state fostered attention on a broader range of issues relating to the social and economic impact of ageing populations (cf. Tibbitts, 1960). The period following the 1940s also saw the development of different theories that explored the relationship between the ageing individual and society, most of which reflected the dominance of functionalist theories within sociology. These drew in particular on the influence of classical sociologists such as Émile Durkheim (1933), who developed the idea of 'organic' solidarity as a feature of modern societies, based around a division of labour that created increasing social heterogeneity and interdependency. Max Weber (1905/1930) was another important influence: his work on bureaucracy and rationalization was applied to research on the emergence of retirement (Donahue et al., 1960). Weber's analysis of the rise of the Protestant ethic in western society was also used to examine the development of leisure and voluntary activities in old age (see, e.g., Kaplan, 1960).

Functionalism, drawing upon Durkheim, Malinowski and others, influenced a range of theoretical approaches to social ageing in the post-war period. From a functionalist perspective, society was viewed as a system with interdependent parts, with all activities and institutions contributing to the maintenance and reproduction of social life (Parsons, 1951). In relation to ageing, functionalists were principally concerned with issues relating to *social integration*, examining the question, 'How can older individuals remain part of society faced with transitions such as retirement, widowhood and long-term illness?'.

At one level, these questions were understood in *structural* terms, with concerns about the impact on older people of changes associated with industrialization and urbanization running alongside increased geographical and social mobility. At the same time, the primary focus was on viewing *individuals* rather than structures as presenting problems, with the task of theories to predict how people could best adjust to the changes associated with modernization alongside ageing populations. Functionalism offered two contrasting responses: first, the need to develop new *social roles* in old age; second, to accept '*disengagement*' as a natural feature of the ageing process.

The first approach – known as role theory – was especially influential in the 1950s and retains, it might be argued, some influence in thinking about ageing as a social process. Functionalists were interested in the impact of the loss of work for men and the potential threats to identity which this might bring. Parsons (1942: 616), for example, summarized the problem thus: 'In view of the very great significance of occupational status and its psychological correlates, retirement leaves the older man in a peculiarly functionless situation, cut-off from participation in the most important activities and interests of society.' Following this, Burgess (1960) viewed elderly people as facing what he termed a 'roleless role', separated from the institutions and relationships that had been important through the individual's life.

From the perspective of role theory, the way to achieve integration in old age was to acquire new roles, whether through re-engaging in work or developing new leisure or related activities. Havighurst (1954: 309), for example, suggested: 'Research has established the fact that activity in a wide variety of social roles is positively related to happiness and good adjustment in old age and also that a high degree of activity in a given social role is positively related to happiness and good social adjustment.'

The relationship between activity and life satisfaction was pursued in a variety of ways during the 1950s and into the 1960s before the theoretical debate was taken over by the publication (in 1961) of Cumming and Henry's *Growing Old: The Process of Disengagement*. The argument developed in that book arose from an empirical study carried out in Kansas City, Missouri, where a panel of people aged 50 and over were selected and interviewed over a number of years. The theory of disengagement was derived from analyses of these interviews. The approach developed was that rather than being concerned about inventing new social roles, we should view old age as a period in which the ageing individual engages with society in a process of mutual separation. A key assumption is that 'ego energy' declines with age and that, as the ageing process develops, individuals become increasingly self-absorbed. It is further argued that disengagement or withdrawal from social relationships will lead to the individual maintaining higher morale in old age – higher, that is, than if he or she attempted to remain involved in a range of social activities. Thus, disengagement is viewed as both a natural and a desirable outcome, one leading to a stronger sense of psychological well-being.

The disengagement hypothesis attracted numerous criticisms and was the subject of considerable debate among social scientists in the 1960s and 1970s working within and beyond the field of ageing. For example, Hochschild (1975), in an influential critique, highlighted what she saw as the 'escape clause' contained within the theory: namely, included in the data were a significant proportion of older people who had *not* withdrawn from society to any noticeable degree. These people were treated by the researchers as either 'unsuccessful' adjusters to old age, 'off-time' disengagers, or members of a 'biological or psychological elite'. Hochschild also noted the way in which the authors conflated a variety of changes in later life, as a result obscuring the contribution that different processes – social, psychological and physical – might make to the experience of growing old. More strident criticisms were also voiced, for example by Blau (1973: 152), who took the view that '[t]he disengagement theory deserves to be publicly attacked, because it can so easily be used as a rationale by the non-old, who constitute the "normals" in society, to avoid confronting and dealing with the issue of old people's marginality and rolelessness in American society'.

Later commentaries focused on the value of the model in developing theoretical debates around the social and social-psychological dimensions of ageing. Daatland (2003) and Lynott and Lynott (1996) suggest that its real significance was in raising awareness of the importance of theory applied to social ageing, and in presenting a systematic approach linking individual ageing to the social system. The ensuing debate also generated new theoretical perspectives (notably in the US), including modernization theory (Cowgill and Holmes, 1972), exchange theory (Dowd, 1975), life course perspectives (Neugarten and Hagestad, 1976), and age stratification theory (Riley et al., 1972). Although they challenge many core assumptions of the disengagement model, these theories furthered the debate about the experience of growing old, applying in the process central concepts from within the social sciences (Lynott and Lynott, 1996).

In the European context, however, use of the disengagement hypothesis as an explicit tool for organizing research was relatively limited. More significant was the use of role theory to interpret empirical findings, with Townsend's (1957) observations about the impact of retirement on working-class men in Bethnal Green a notable example. Role and disengagement theory were, however, important (and certainly influential) in reinforcing a view that growing old represented a significant degree of *discontinuity* from prior life events and experiences. Physical and mental changes were seen to bring processes of decline and mental inflexibility. At the same time, the pace of economic and cultural change was viewed as limiting the value of older people's contribution to the social system – views which Townsend (1981) was to summarize as a form of 'acquiescent functionalism' and which featured prominently in the modernization theory as propounded by Cowgill and Holmes (1972).

Equally characteristic, however, was the absence of any consideration of the impact of social structure in determining the lives of older people. Marshall (1986: 12) highlighted this point where he noted the emphasis of studies in the 1950s and 1960s on the 'adjustment of the individual to the society'. He went on to observe:

> Whether measured by degree of social integration or more psychological variables such as morale and life satisfaction, the adjustment of the ageing individual became the dependent variable of choice for hundreds of investigations [during this period]. No equivalent measure of conceptualization of the 'adjustment' of the society to the individual ever gained prominence in the research armamentarium of gerontology. Even disengagement theory, which did attempt to provide a theory linking the individual and societal levels of analysis, in practice stimulated research focused on individual ageing people and their adjustment to society. Social change or the social dynamics surrounding disengagement have rarely been addressed in this theoretical tradition.

The next phase of theorizing begins to address a number of the above issues, notably in attempts to engage with age and its relationship with social structure, and later with studies of the relationship between individual biographies and historical events and their influence through the life course (Elder, 1974). More generally, we find a rejection from the 1970s onwards of attempts to build general theories of ageing or changes covering all points of what came increasingly to be termed as 'the life course'. John (1984: 92) summarized this position as follows: 'To the extent that one can characterize theoretical developments . . . the trend has been away from a search for a special as well as a universal theory of aging. It is wise to abandon these endeavors since any effort along these lines will remain fruitless as long as material and ideal conditions vary from country to country'.

Social theory and social change

The period from the 1970s through to the 1980s represents a complex series of changes in the position of older people. There is a gradual shift – uneven in timing across Europe and the US – away from perspectives which viewed ageing primarily as a 'social problem'. From the late 1960s new theories were introduced, drawing upon symbolic interactionism, revisions to existing approaches (such as activity and role theory), psychological models such as socio-emotional selectivity theory, theories of the life course, and political economy perspectives (Estes, 1979; Marshall, 1986; Passuth and Bengtson, 1996; Baltes and Baltes, 1990). Increasingly, attempts are made to move beyond an individual-level focus with attempts to combine macro- and micro-sociological approaches (Riley, 1987).

This shift in theorizing reflected broader currents within the social sciences, with the questioning of functionalist perspectives (see especially Gouldner, 1971) and the rise of phenomenological and Marxist theories (Estes et al., 2003). In contrast with previous theories which had focused on the idea of ageing as a period of *discontinuity* from previous life phases, emphasis was placed on *continuity* with earlier periods of the life course (Atchley, 2000). This might arise through being a member of a particular birth cohort, or through the influence of statuses associated with class, gender and ethnicity, or through developing certain lifestyles and interests.

The first major theoretical perspective in this phase – *age stratification theory* – drew strongly on the functionalist tradition but, at the same time, provided a link to future theories with its emphasis on birth cohorts and life course perspectives. Crucially, as a theoretical model, it took the debate beyond individual adjustment towards issues focusing on the influence of social structure. Age stratification theory examined the influence of social structures on the process of individual ageing and the stratification of age in society (Riley and Riley, 1994). Members of different cohorts are viewed as comprising 'age strata' (i.e., children, middle-aged adults, older people), among whom differences may be counted both in terms of age and also in respect to the historical experiences to which they have been exposed (Riley, 1987). Two important arguments follow from this type of approach: first, that age is an important mechanism for *regulating* behaviour through the life course, determining as a result access to positions of power and life chances more generally; second, that birth cohorts themselves play an influential role in the process of social change. Riley (1987: 4) argues: 'As society moves through time, the age strata of people and roles are altered. The people in particular age strata are no longer the *same* people: they have been replaced by younger entrants from more recent cohorts, with more recent life experiences.'

Age stratification theory provided valuable insights into the complexity of age as a variable within the social structure. But the limitations of the approach were also important, with three issues identified in the literature: first, the way that it overemphasized the role of age status in the distribution of economic and social rewards; second, the lack of attention to social and economic differences within birth cohorts; third, the retention of functionalist assumptions regarding consensus as regards the structure and operation of social systems and institutions.

The next important theory which moved beyond individual adjustment to ageing (and which also drew upon arguments from age stratification) was the *life course* perspective (Elder, 1974; Neugarten and Hagestad, 1976). With this theory, ageing individuals and cohorts are viewed in terms of one phase of the entire lifetime, influenced by historical, social, economic and environmental factors that occur at earlier ages. Passuth and Bengtson (1996: 17) summarize the key elements of the approach: '[1] aging occurs from birth to death (thereby distinguishing this theory from those that focus exclusively on the elderly); [2] aging involves social, psychological and biological processes; and [3] aging experiences are shaped by cohort-historical factors.'

The above illustration further emphasizes the influence of birth cohorts both on the construction of the life course and on the experience of ageing itself. Instead of generalizing, for instance, about the characteristics of 70-year-olds per se, we can see that 70-year-olds who were born in 1890 are in many ways different from 70-year-olds who were born in 1930. In other words, cross-sectional data cannot be relied upon to construct or predict life course patterns. This discovery of cohort differences helped to undermine the idea that ageing could be a universal, biologically driven process which would work in much the same way in all times and all places. Against this, ageing appeared to vary according to different social, cultural and historical contexts.

Dannefer and Settersten (2010) suggest that models of the life course break down into two main paradigms. The first they term *personological*, defined as the attempt to use key features of early life experiences to predict and account for outcomes in late life. This approach is best illustrated through the work of Glen Elder, whose study *Children of the Great Depression* (1974) demonstrated the extent to which social conditions during childhood and youth could have a lasting impact on the individual's subsequent psychological and social development. The second paradigm – called *institutional* – does not focus on the individual, but views the life course as a social and political construct comprising age-graded stages organized though social institutions and social policy (Kohli, 1986). With this approach, emphasis is placed on the way in which 'age-based' norms influence the organization of the life course, defining 'age-appropriate' points for full-time education, leaving home, work and retirement.

Both these paradigms have undoubted strengths for understanding social processes underpinning the social construction of ageing. However, important criticisms have also been raised, highlighting the complex sociological questions involved in understanding ageing. For example, in relation to the personological approach, Dannefer and Kelly-Moore (2009) identify what they term the 'Time 1 Problem', which refers to the practice of predicting later-life outcomes by measuring environmental factors only at the initial observation period, leaving change at subsequent time periods as a given. For example, in relation to Elder's work, it is difficult to be sure whether hardships experienced early in life and psychological functioning in later life have a direct causal link, or whether experiences (in work and in the family) in intervening years are more important. What seems probable is that any convincing explanation of events over the life course will require linkages between events in childhood and practices and processes in adulthood itself, recognizing the extent to which change is likely to take place at least as much within as between birth cohorts (Kelly-Moore and Lin, 2011).

In relation to the institutional paradigm, this has particular strengths in highlighting the way in which social markers of different kinds play a significant role shaping movement through the life course. Equally significant has been the recognition of the importance of what has been termed *chronologization* (see Chapter 3) – the influence of age and time – as a major dimension affecting the organization of daily life. But although this model has considerable descriptive power, the underlying social and economic forces driving changes to the life course are left unclear. Thus arguments about a destandardized life course have been the focus of considerable debate (see Chapter 4), but the factors shaping this development (in particular those associated with globalization and deindustrialization) are poorly integrated into life course perspectives. At the same time, the institutional paradigm leaves unresolved the long-run debate within sociology about the relationship between structure and agency (see, especially, Giddens, 1994; Sewell, 1992) and, in particular, tension between individuals behaving as purposeful actors as contrasted with the idea of a socially regulated life course. In response, researchers such as Settersten (1999) have emphasized an 'agency within structure' perspective, highlighting how individuals both shape as well as have their lives changed by social structure. Similarly, Marshall and Clarke (2010) put forward a 'duality of structure' approach that combines agency with a view of structures as holding resources that influence and have bearing upon intentional behaviour.

Ageing as a social construction

From the 1980s through to the 2000s, research on social aspects of ageing began to embrace a variety of perspectives, with important contributions from feminism, social history, political economy and developmental psychology. In some cases, as Katz (2003: 16) observes, studies began to incorporate areas that were – from the 1990s at least – losing ground elsewhere in the social sciences (the influence of Marxism in the development of critical gerontology is one such example). In other instances, researchers drew upon perspectives within mainstream sociology, for example work associated with Foucault (Powell and Chamberlain (2012) and Bourdieu (Gilleard and Higgs, 2005).

The difference between this period and previous ones is that no single theory was especially dominant, although political economy (subsequently critical gerontology) assumed major significance during the 1980s and 1990s (Estes et al., 2003). The precursor of critical gerontology can be seen in a number of approaches grouped under the heading of the 'social construction of ageing', an important theme developed in research from the late 1970s onwards (Estes, 1979; Phillipson, 1982; Gubrium, 1986). In an initial formulation of this approach, Estes (1979: 1) argued:

> The major problems faced by the elderly in the United States are in large measure ones that are socially constructed as a result of our conceptions of aging and the aged. What is done for and about the elderly, as well as what we know about them, including knowledge gained from research, are products of our conceptions of aging. In an important sense, then, the major problems faced by the elderly are the ones we create for them.

The processes of social construction are viewed as occurring at all levels; the state and the economy (macro level) influence the experience and condition of ageing, while individuals also actively construct their worlds through personal interactions (micro level) and through organizational and institutional structures and processes (meso level) that constitute their daily social worlds and society itself.

At the micro and the meso levels, sociologists examined the various social contexts through which ageing was constructed. Gubrium (1986), for example, focused on the issue of Alzheimer's disease, looking at the way in which the meaning of the illness is derived and communicated. He uses the example of support groups for people with Alzheimer's to show how these can provide a basis for speaking about and interpreting the caregiving experience. For Gubrium, the 'local cultures' of residential settings, day centres and support groups provide important contexts for working through and assigning meanings to particular experiences. In this approach, language is seen to play a crucial role in the construction of reality. Lynott and Lynott (1996: 754) summarize this approach as follows:

> Instead of asking how things like age cohorts, life stages, or system needs organise and determine one's experience, [the question is] how persons (professional and lay alike) make use of age-related explanations and justifications in their treatment and interaction with one another . . . Facts virtually come to life in their assertion, invocation, realization and utility. From this point of view, language is not just a vehicle for symbolically representing realities; its usage, in the practical realities of everyday life, is concretely productive of the realities.

Estes (1981: 400) took the view that the social construction of reality approach – building upon the original theories of Berger and Luckmann (1967) and the labelling theory perspective of Becker (1963) and Matza (1964) – offered several insights for understanding social aspects of ageing:

> The experience of old age is dependent in large part upon how others react to the aged; that is social context and cultural meanings are important. Meanings are crucial in influencing how growing old is experienced . . . in any given society; these meanings are shaped through interaction of the aged with the individuals, organizations, and institutions that comprise the social context. Social context, however, incorporates not only situational events and interactional opportunities but also structural constraints that limit the range of possible interaction and the degree of understanding, reinforcing certain lines of action while barring others.

By the end of the 1980s, some of the themes associated with the social construction approach had coalesced into the idea of a 'critical gerontology', building first on work in political economy but subsequently extending to research in the humanities.[1] At the same time, earlier theoretical approaches such as life course perspectives continued to develop, notably around issues relating to social inequality in old age. The context for this work as well as some of its main themes, form the next section of this chapter.

Social ageing and social inequality

From the 1980s onwards, perceptions of ageing populations as representing a threat to western economies became widespread (World Bank, 1994; Mullan, 2000). With this came questioning of those sections of the welfare state targeted at older people, notably in relation to areas such as expenditure on pensions and social security. At the same time, the institutionalization of retirement – underpinned by earlier withdrawal from work on the one side and extended life expectancy on the other – also came under scrutiny. Increasingly, western governments were urging older people to remain in the workforce for as long as possible, reinforced by the raising of the state pension age (Vickerstaff et al., 2011). Alongside this came anxieties about what was viewed as the burden represented by public pensions and the financial pressures likely to be faced by succeeding generations (Willetts, 2010). At the same time, the debate about demography moved from national to global contexts, with influential international governmental organizations (IGOs) such as the World Bank, the International Monetary Fund and the World Trade Organization contributing to what was termed the 'crisis construction and crisis management of old age' (Estes and Associates, 2001).

Research around social inequality was reflected in an extension of the life course model (Dannefer, 2003) and in further development of political economy perspectives on ageing (Baars et al., 2006). The former is illustrated in the development of the cumulative advantage and disadvantage (CAD) model through the work of researchers such as O'Rand (2000), Crystal and Shea (2003) and Dannefer (2003). This approach focuses on growing old as a collective process of intra-cohort stratification, as social processes allow the accumulation of advantages over the life course for some, but the accretion of disadvantages for others.

The specific contribution of studies of ageing and the life course to understanding social inequalities is to demonstrate the tendency for the latter to become more pronounced during the process of ageing. In the CAD paradigm the popular expression "The rich get richer, the poor get poorer" is linked with social processes of differentiation over the life course. Instead of portraying the aged as poor and dependent on inadequate pension arrangements or claiming that everyone in the baby boom generation will be much better off in comparison with younger generations, the approach identifies life course trajectories (and points of vulnerability within these) that widen inequalities from midlife onwards. Elements of the CAD paradigm can be found in Marxist class analysis (Estes, 1979), feminist perspectives (Estes, 2006) as well as aspects of continuity theory (Atchley, 2000).

Crystal (2006) has argued that although early advantages and disadvantages, such as parental status and formal education, have long and persisting influences, it is the resources and events characteristic of the midlife period that have a direct bearing upon later-life economic and health status. He observes:

> By midlife . . . the relationship between the economic and health domains becomes more apparent. The cumulative consequences of differences in socioeconomic status on health are often long term in nature; they become more marked in midlife after decades of exposure to differential stresses and risks. Disparities are generated through multiple pathways, including socioeconomic differences in risky health behaviours; differences in access to health care . . . ; and differences in occupational stress and occupationally based coping resources. (2006: 207)

Issues of inequality have also been a preoccupation of the political economy approach within critical gerontology (Phillipson, 1998; Estes et al., 2003; Baars et al., 2006). Early work in this area focused upon the various elements contributing to what Townsend (1981; 1986) referred to as the 'structured dependency' of later life, defined as a product of forced exclusion from the labour market, passive forms of community care and the impact of poverty (see also Estes, 1979). This initial focus on dependency broadened out in three main ways during the 1980s and 1990s: first, in relation to research on social inequality; second, in studies on the role of the state in the production of dependency; third, in relation to the influencing of globalization on ageing.

Social class became a major concern in respect of the first of the above, reflecting the influence of Marxism within the political economy model (Walker and Foster, 2006). In parallel with the CAD approach, political economy theorists took the view that older people were as deeply divided along class (and other social) fault lines as younger and middle-aged adults. Walker (1996: 33) contrasted this approach with functionalist theories that tended to view age as erasing class and status differentials. He argued:

> There is no doubt that the process of retirement, not ageing, does superimpose reduced socio-economic status on a majority of older people . . . but even so retirement has a differential impact on older people, depending on their prior socio-economic status. For example, there is unequal access to occupational pensions. Women and other groups with incomplete employment records are particularly disadvantaged . . .There are also inequalities between generations of older people, arising from . . . unequal access to . . . private and occupational pension provision.

Social class also re-emerged as an important variable as researchers focused upon intra- as well as inter-cohort analysis. Cohort-level analysis had been especially important in demonstrating the extent to which patterns of ageing could vary over time, allowing researchers to challenge ideas about later life having a 'normative' or 'natural' trajectory. Nonetheless, emphasis on cohort experiences of ageing neglected the extent of inequalities (especially those relating to social class) *within* particular birth cohorts. Dannefer and Kelly-Moore (2009: 393) make the following point: 'Thus while the analytic tactic of comparing cohorts demonstrated the *importance* of context, it also allowed cohorts to stand as virtually *coterminous* with context so that the role of social forces operating within each context (e.g. regulating heterogeneity and homogeneity) received little attention.'

The move back to focusing on the role of social structure within cohorts provided a way of recognizing the importance of social class as a factor generating inequalities through the life course. This was not, it might be argued, entirely incompatible with ideas associated with what were viewed as trends towards 'individualization' (Beck, 1992), the development of new identities associated with what came to be characterized as 'the third age' (Laslett, 1989) and the importance of consumption for those from the baby-boom cohort (Jones et al., 2008; Gilleard and Higgs, 2011). Notwithstanding these developments, social class has continued to play a significant role in influencing life chances in older age – even more so given the growth of inequalities which have followed periods of economic growth and subsequent recession in western economies (Dorling, 2011).

An additional concern of political economy, again reflecting the Marxist legacy, was attention to the role of the state as representing a site of class struggle and for managing the affairs of dominant class interests (O'Connor, 1973). The study of the state was viewed as central to understanding old age and the life chances of older people since it had the power (a) to allocate and distribute scarce resources to ensure survival and growth of the economy, (b) to mediate the different segments and classes of society and (c) to ameliorate social conditions that could threaten the existing order. Estes (1999: 23) argued that a key task for political economy was to analyse 'the aged and state policy intrinsic to part of the broader phenomenon of crisis construction and management in advanced capitalism and [to] consider ... how the aged and [policies towards older people] are used in this process.'

Globalization and inequality

The influence of social class must also be positioned within the context of the complex changes introduced by globalization and the potential of these to enhance inequalities based around class, gender and ethnicity. Debates around the impact of globalization on ageing have been extensive both within the social gerontology literature (see, for example, Baars et al., 2006; Dannefer and Phillipson, 2010) and in studies of social welfare (George and Wilding, 2002; Yeates, 2001). One argument emerging from within gerontology concerns the extent to which globalization has itself become an influential factor in the construction of old age, notably in the design of policies aimed at regulating and managing population ageing. Although the impact of globalization remains 'highly contested' (Diamond, 2010), there seems no question that an interdependent world such as that associated with more fluid labour markets and transnational forms of governance creates distinctive pressures and influences across the life course. Much work has still to be done in working out more precisely what these might be and the relative influences on the particular policies of national and global actors. Yeates (2001: 2) suggests, for example, that the relationship between globalization and social policy is best conceived as 'dialectical' or 'reciprocal', and that 'far from states, welfare states and populations passively "receiving" [and] adapting to globalization . . . they are active participants in its development'. This may be especially the case in the context of the present economic recession where the role of nation-states in managing the crisis, over and against global bodies, appears to have been enhanced (Gray, 2010).

The processes associated with globalization have assisted the development of a new approach to ageing societies, based around what Ferge (1997b) refers to as the 'individualization of the social'. On the one side, ageing is presented as a global problem and concern; on the other, the focus has moved towards individualizing the various risks attached to growing old. In this context, Young (1999: 6) has interpreted such developments as part of a wider shift:

> [from an] *inclusive* to an *exclusive* society. That is from a society whose accent was on assimilation and incorporation to one that separates and excludes. This erosion of the inclusive world . . . involved processes of disaggregation both in the sphere of community (the rise of individualism) and the sphere of work (transformation of . . . labour markets). Both processes are the result of market forces and their transformation by the human actors involved.

From a sociological perspective, however, writers such as Bauman (1998) have presented the 'human consequences' of globalization in terms of new forms of exclusion and segregation, especially affecting those in deprived and peripheral communities. And Sennett (2006) linked aspects of globalization – for example the rise of flexible labour markets – to the 'erosion of social capitalism', with older workers increasingly disadvantaged within corporations that emphasized low-wage and low-skill work environments.

All of the above carries significant implications for under-standing the landscape of social class and social inequality in later life. The impact of globalization, alongside and interact-ing with a transformed life course, has redefined the social context of ageing. Population ageing has now to be 'managed' within what has been described as a fluid and deregulated social order (Elliott and Lemert, 2006), thus opening the pos-sibility for class inequalities to find new forms of expression. Risks once carried by social institutions have now been dis-placed onto the shoulders of individuals and/or their families. Dannefer (2000: 270) summarizes this process in the follow-ing way: 'Corporate and state uncertainties are transferred to citizens – protecting large institutions while exposing indi-viduals to possible catastrophe in the domains of health care and personal finances, justified to the public by the claim that the pensioner can do better on his or her own.' At the same time, the evidence suggests widening inequalities within and between different countries, produced as a consequence of global forces. Rather than leading inexorably to minimum levels of social protection (Mosley and Uno, 2007), globaliza-tion has been implicated in the rise in income inequality produced as a consequence of falling relative demand for unskilled labour and the weakened power of labour organiza-tions (Glyn, 2007). The increase in incomes at the very top of the income distribution was a feature of advanced indus-trial societies throughout the 1990s and 2000s (Judt, 2010). For those less fortunate, however, there was the growth of what Sennett (2006) refers to as 'underemployment', which comes with constraints on wages and salaries, both of which run alongside the contraction of jobs that accompanies eco-nomic globalization (see further Blossfield et al., 2006). All these developments have transformed the experience of growing old, introducing new forms of social and economic inequality into the experience of everyday life.

Reconstructing later life: Consumption and the rise of the 'third age'

Although critical gerontology has continued to explore, as argued above, issues relating to the impact of various forms of inequality, another theoretical approach has been to view ageing as being transformed by a new generation entering later life with issues relating to the consumption of material and related goods forming a prominent place in the organization of social life. Drawing on the work of Bourdieu and Foucault, writers such as Gilleard and Higgs (2000; 2005) have challenged the extent to which 'structured dependency' or issues relating to poverty and inequality provide a meaningful basis for understanding the experiences of older people. As an alternative, Bourdieu's (1977) concepts of 'habitus' and 'field' are used to illustrate that the way in which we think about issues relating to 'cohorts' and 'generations' needs to be reframed. These are not merely, it is argued, aggregates of individuals born at a certain point in time; rather, they are a group 'emerging at a particular moment in history, distributed through a new mass culture' (Jones et al., 2008: 34). Essentially, this is a culture driven by 'mass consumption' to which the new (baby boom) generation have made a major contribution throughout their life course. According to Higgs and Gilleard (2010: 1440), 'the "generational habitus" of the present-day cohort of older people has been shaped by consumption practices that ran in tandem with the benefits of the "Golden Age" of welfare and its concomitant mass affluence'.

This argument is linked to the idea – following Laslett (1989) – that it is now possible to identify what might be termed a 'third age' in between that of work (the 'second age') and late old age (the 'fourth age') which opens up the possibilities for new forms of personal development. Ageing, from this perspective, rather than a period of 'dependency' or 'decline', is better viewed as a period of flexibility and choice. Identities – notably for the baby boom generation – rather than built around the narrow platform of work or production, are increasingly formed around consumption and the pursuit of commodities. Jones et al. (2008: 114) draw the conclusion that:

> it is possible to consider the third age in late modernity as a cultural field where later life becomes more diverse and heterogenous. Within the context of a post-scarcity westernised life course, it is no longer appropriate to categorise people entering later life as a homogenous group of 'retirees', 'third

agers' or indeed 'pensioners'. Instead post-working life is based around a variety of lifestyles, uncertainties, anxieties and aspirations. Furthermore, the cultural field that comprises the 'third age' transcends social distinctions based around age, class, status, race or gender. The crucial underpinning to this cultural field is the rise of mass consumer society . . . [and] the transformation of consumption practices that successive generations take with them into later life.

This theoretical focus on the importance of consumption in underpinning post-work identities represents a significant departure from perspectives discussed elsewhere in this chapter. It has played an important role in highlighting the possibility for people to shape their own 'ageing' in a way which was inconceivable for previous generations. And the idea of a 'third age' of freedom from the constraints of paid employment undoubtedly carries many attractions. But we shall also note in later chapters many limitations to this approach. People reaching retirement age today have indeed been 'exposed to and [have] participated in an expanding consumer market' (Jones et al., 2008: 25). However, it is precisely this biographical experience that may create considerable frustrations and anxieties given the financial pressures now affecting those moving into later life – not least in the field of pensions and social care (see further Chapters 6 and 8). Moreover, the idea of a 'third age' which transcends that of class, gender and ethnicity is itself difficult to substantiate; indeed all the evidence – as will again be explored in this book – points the other way. Nonetheless, the idea of people choosing to manage and control their own ageing is important, even while requiring significant social interventions if it is to be realized. We shall return to this particular issue in the final two chapters of this book.

Conclusion

Looking ahead over the next decade, what are the likely challenges affecting sociological theory as applied to the study of ageing? A continuing challenge will be how to maintain social theory as a valid and significant activity within research that studies the lives of older people. On the one side, it is possible to look back upon a productive period of some 60 years of theorizing – from theories of social adjustment in old age in the 1940s (Pollak, 1948) to perspectives on globalization and ageing at the beginning of the twenty-first century (Dannefer and Phillipson, 2010). Theory continues to be used to try to make sense both of the issues that confront older people in their daily lives, and of the choice and dilemmas for society in resolving their questions and concerns. But the status and value of theory need constantly to be reaffirmed against pressures to restrict the study of social ageing either to the evaluation of public policies or to the enumeration of the conditions associated with being an older person. Hagestad and Dannefer (2001: 4) view this as part of what they suggest is a 'persistent tendency towards microfication in social sciences approaches to aging'. They argue:

> Microfication refers to a trend in the substantive issues and analytic foci, what we might call the ontology of social research in aging. Increasingly, attention has been concentrated on psycho-social characteristics of individuals in micro-interactions, to the neglect of the macrolevel. Apart from the population characteristics, macrolevel phenomena of central interest to social scientists, such as social institutions, cohesion and conflict, norms and values, have slipped out of focus.

A major challenge for the foreseeable future will be to continue to evolve macro-level theories which make sense of the increasing complexity of the links between ageing, on the one side, and social structure, on the other. Indeed, it is precisely the intricacy of these relationships that demand coherent social theories to be developed, continuing to acknowledge ageing both as a lived, individual experience as well as one constructed through social, cultural and economic relationships. For this to take place, however, important changes will need to be made to the way in which theory develops within gerontology. Daatland (2003: 7) highlights what he sees as the 'relative isolation of gerontology from basic disciplines like psychology and sociology – or for that matter, like economics, anthropology, and history'. One outcome of this has been – especially in the case of Europe – the limited range of theory drawn into gerontology, much of it lagging behind developments in the major social science disciplines. In some respects, this has begun to change with the wide range of influences drawn upon by critical gerontology – from the humanities, feminism, critical theory and mainstream sociology. But much social gerontology remains distinctly atheoretical in approach, continuing to use theory as an *implicit* rather than an *explicit* medium for testing ideas and hypotheses.

Producing coherent theory in gerontology may also require greater attention to some of the disadvantages as well as the advantages of the interdisciplinary form of the gerontological enterprise. The idea of interdisciplinarity is viewed as a major feature of studies of ageing, with researchers pointing to the virtues of crossing boundaries both within the social sciences and across to the natural sciences and humanities. This has led to some significant developments in theoretical work – for example, in ideas about successful ageing (Baltes and Baltes, 1990) and in the evolution of critical gerontology (Moody, 1988). On the one hand, the problems attached to interdisciplinary working should also be noted. Daatland (2003: 8), for example, refers to gerontology as being 'trapped in the cage of interdisciplinarity', and notes:

> Most established disciplines and universities resist such an effort, which, while it may be an advantage when you want to solve practical problems, may be a drawback when you develop theories. Theories are more or less by their nature discipline-specific; in fact they may even refer to sub-disciplines within each discipline.

The solution to this problem will not be to abandon interdisciplinary research – which has in any event great virtues in fields such as ageing – rather, it must be to engage in such work from the standpoint of greater confidence about discipline-specific theoretical standpoints. Thus, gerontological work in geography, psychology and sociology, to take three examples, must achieve closer integration with mainstream developments within those disciplines. This must be viewed as a precondition both for developing both new types of theory as well as creating more effective forms of interdisciplinary activity.

Despite the obstacles identified above, much has been achieved in the sixty-year span of theorizing about the nature of ageing individuals and ageing societies. The immediate future for older people poses new risks in the context of financial insecurities and instabilities across a global stage. These also provide a fresh justification – if one were needed – for theories to address both the changes in the way individuals experience later life and alterations in the social relations which underpin growing old. Achieving a secure identity given the risks associated with late modernity will be a major task for older people in the future. Sociological and social psychological theories must continue to evolve to assist understanding about how individuals and social institutions respond to this challenge. Moreover, theories themselves are essential for understanding the power of different definitions of 'age' in influencing behaviour and the way in which such definitions form and take shape within social institutions. It is a discussion of this particular theme that forms the subject of the next chapter of this book.

4

The Development of Ideas About Age and Ageing

Introduction

The purpose of this chapter is to provide an introduction to thinking about ageing from a sociological perspective, drawing upon the demographic and theoretical context explored in the previous two chapters. For a variety of reasons this task presents us with an important challenge. In the first place, the idea of 'age' – and especially 'old age' – comes with historical baggage. There is, in particular, a view about the existence of a 'golden age', which offered greater security and safety for older people, who were well treated by their families and whose productive roles were maintained until the end of life was reached. This broad view of how people were treated in previous historical periods – apart from being inaccurate in much of the detail – has had the cumulative effect of treating 'the old' in recent times as a homogenous 'other', set apart from and viewed as disadvantaged exclusively on the basis of their age.

A second and linked challenge is a set of assumptions about ageing itself which views it as a 'natural' event unfolding in a predetermined fashion as the individual moves from birth to death. Ageing is seen as an immutable process affecting humans – something which can be defined as part of a characteristic pattern of events, or 'normal ageing' as it is sometimes described. In contrast with this approach, an alternative view presents ageing as something which can only be understood in its relationship with the 'social' – especially relationships, institutions and resources. This is not to say that age as a category on its own is unimportant in our lives. On the contrary, we have a strong sense of age-appropriate behaviours and of passing through age-related transitions – stages even. But these behaviours and transitions are, it will be argued, best understood as 'socially-determined' (in the broadest sense) events – i.e., our concern is with the social creation of 'age' and the institutions and behaviours with which it is associated. This point will be developed in different ways in this book. This chapter provides a historical survey of the development of ideas about age and ageing. Chapter 5 examines the social construction of ageing through the twentieth century up until the present time. In Part II, the development of ageing populations will be illustrated in the context of the inequalities and divisions characteristic of societies in the twenty-first century.

Perspectives on age and ageing

Already in this book, terms such as 'age', 'ageing' and 'older people' have been used somewhat interchangeably. Lack of precision in the use of such terms reflects both the absence of an agreed language for describing the older population and the fact that the boundaries surrounding ageing remain fluid, with existing definitions building upon historical tradition, cultural influences and personal choice (Thane, 2000). In western societies it is also the case that many of the terms and categories used to describe ageing and old age reflect the preoccupations of those concerned with elderly people as a 'problem' category. As a result, there is a tendency to focus upon questions of size ('more' older people), or a particular category (the 'very elderly'), or a certain condition (people with 'dementia' or a 'disability').

Of course, categories are important and, indeed, necessary in many cases for developing appropriate policies. Yet they also have limitations, often resulting in a distorted view of the capacities of people, especially if based upon selective use of available facts and experiences. The danger which follows is to view people of a 'certain age' only in terms of their diseases and disabilities. The tendency is to emphasize issues such as poverty, bereavement and loneliness. Against this, elderly people who fail to fit what has been termed a pathology model of ageing (e.g. the fit, those who are active, those with wealth, the assertive, anyone getting on with a purposeful life) are defined out of existence. They are not a problem, they have no obvious needs; as a consequence, they cannot really be 'elderly'.

In contrast with the above approach, the point of a sociological perspective is precisely to take a broader view of the lives of people in the period known as old age. Sociologists adopt a contrasting approach to ageing in comparison with other social science disciplines. The sociologist starts from the view that old age is interesting because – although it is an enduring human phenomenon handled differently by different societies – it is at the same time changing and influencing human behaviour. The sociologist is concerned to explore the processes involved and how they are being interpreted by men and women from different social classes, ethnic groups and cultural settings. This approach contrasts with social policy and government interests in old age. In these contexts, old age is regarded as a problem (for the economy or the health service, to take two examples) – hence the need for some analysis and collection of data. This approach has its own validity and justification, but it often leads to a distorted view of social ageing, together with a limited selection of topics to be analysed and discussed.

Sociological perspectives emphasize (as noted in the previous chapter) a broad definition of the relationship between age and society. Rather than old age as such, interest is typically focused on ageing within the context of the *life course*, the latter expressing the movement of individuals through time and through socially defined transitions such as adolescence, midlife and retirement. Matilda White Riley, an influential figure in American sociology, refers to the *interdependence* of ageing on the one side and society on the other. She makes the important point that in studying age, we not only bring people back into society, but recognize that *both* people and society undergo process and change: 'The aim is to understand each of the two dynamisms: (1) the *aging of people* in successive cohorts who grow up, grow old, die, and are replaced by other people; and (2) the *changes in society* as people of different ages pass through the social institutions that are organized by age' (Riley, 1987: 2).

The above arguments raise important issues about how our understanding of ideas associated with age and ageing have evolved over time. The various sections of this chapter explore this issue, tracing changes in approaches to age from premodern times until the beginning of the twentieth century.

Understanding age and ageing

John Macnicol (2006: 3) makes the point that, at every stage of our lives, we are confronted by the inevitability of our own ageing: 'As we progress through the "journey of life", we are acutely conscious of the ageing process as it affects our bodies, our attitudes, the environment we create for ourselves and our interactions with people of different ages.' Indeed, it might be argued that in the twenty-first century, at least in high-income societies, we have become acutely conscious of the changes which seem to accompany ageing – hence the rise of an 'anti-ageing' medicine designed to slow or even reverse physical changes affecting the body. And societies – for the demographic reasons outlined in the previous chapter – are more aware of the clustering of particular groups identified as being of a certain 'age' with concerns expressed about the disadvantages (though less commonly the advantages) which this might bring.

But with the above in mind, two points must be emphasized: first, age as a social category has always been subject to diverse social and cultural interpretations – these often changing with great rapidity under particular social and economic influences. Second, that related categories – such as old age – also cover widely varying circumstances, especially when applied to a broad spectrum of chronological ages such as those stretching from 60 to 100. Thane (2000) emphasizes, on the one side, the historical variability of definitions of old age, which depend upon the appearance and physical capacities of individuals. One the other, what has been the gradual consolidation of 'official' definitions of an 'older person', with the age of 60 an important turning point in how people are viewed and the duties they are expected to perform.

The idea of people passing through different ages and stages of life is itself deeply rooted in western culture, illustrated in the writings of Aristotle, Dante, Shakespeare and many others. In the Middle Ages, descriptions of the journey of life were organized around three, four, five or seven ages, depending on the principle (e.g. biological, astrological) involved (Burrow, 1986). Moody (2010: 4) notes that this presentation of the human life cycle balanced the image of ages or stages with the idea of life as a spiritual pilgrimage: 'From that standpoint, no period of life could be viewed as superior to another. Just as the natural life cycle was orientated by the recurrent cycle of the seasons, so the individual soul could be orientated toward the hope of an afterlife.' Minois (1989: 161), however, viewing the period from the eleventh to the fourteenth century, questions whether these early representations of life's journey had much influence beyond the educated (largely religious) elite. In medieval times one was 'young' or 'old': 'young so long as one retained one's physical strength, old as soon as it started to decline'. Minois concludes:

> So long as physical incapacity had not totally paralysed the individual, no difference at all was made between the mature man and the old man, who retained his place in society until he went into retirement, which he did only in the last extremity. Dividing up the 'ages of life' was an intellectual game which did not correspond to any reality in fact or in law. Human life was one and indivisible. It began at baptism and ended with the tomb. (1989: 207)

Cole (1992: 110–111) suggests that new models of the life course – represented in the image of a pyramid of stairs – emerged in Northern Europe in the sixteenth and seventeenth centuries, and continued to evolve through the eighteenth and nineteenth centuries (see Figures 4.1 and 4.2). Early representations remained wedded to a vision of life dominated by birth, marriage and death with only limited space for an old

Figure 4.1 'The Life and Age of Woman: Stages of Woman's Life, from the Cradle to the Grave', by James Baillie, *c*.1848
Source: Wikimedia Commons, US Library of Congress Prints and Photographs Division

Figure 4.2 'The Life and Age of Man: Stages of Man's Life, from the Cradle to the Grave', by James Baillie, *c*.1848
Source: Wikimedia Commons, US Library of Congress Prints and Photographs Division

age with distinctive needs or obligations. Old age may, in this regard, have been a 'stage in life', but it was not one which attracted any particular expectations on the part of either the older person or society. In its earliest form, the image of the rising and falling staircase was itself embedded in a religious iconography linking behaviour in the present life with that after death. Cole (1992: 25) describes this as follows:

> Sixteenth-century examples of the motif depicted a balance between life and death, sacred and secular. Though the timing of death was uncertain and judgment loomed ahead, the fabric of a pious life, woven together with good manners . . . and faith in God, promised eternal salvation. Although the staircase motif clearly favoured the secular power and productivity of middle age, ageing still implied an uncertain journey to eternal life.

As suggested in the above quotation, early versions of the pyramid represented 'middle age' as the apex or crown of life, when life's achievements were brought together and celebrated. After this point, the dominant image was that of decline and decrepitude. Botelho (2005: 119) cites a description of the decades of life popular in Germany in the sixteenth century and one which may have been familiar still in the seventeenth (see Table 4.1).

The focus on middle age as demonstrated in Table 4.1 reflects greater emphasis placed in the sixteenth to the

Table 4.1 Decades of life

10 years – a child
20 years – youth
30 years – a man
40 years – standing still
50 years – settled and prosperous
60 years – departing
70 years – protect your soul
80 years – the world's fool
90 years – the scorn of children
100 years – God have mercy

Source: Botelho, 2005: 119

eighteenth century on social markers linked to numerical age. Thomas (1976: 248) suggests that in the case of English society, stratification by age increased over this period, with the anomalies of youthful advancement reduced and the redundancy of the old given greater prominence. He concludes: 'Culturally inherited milestones such as the two key ages at 21 and 60 took on a new importance. Indeed, it could be said that full humanity was often confined to persons between those two ages.' Gilleard and Higgs (2010: 123) note the change in the late Middle Ages from viewing old age as a 'spiritually-valued stage in life' to an administrative category worthy of support from the state. They suggest that one consequence of this development was to 'shift the earlier moral categorization of old age to a socially constructed one – represented in the first instance by formalizing provision for the aged as part of the deserving poor'.

The above change reflects a broader transformation from linking old age to religious destiny and fate, to secular concerns with securing a decent existence in the present life. Religious themes became less dominant in approaches to ageing. The influence of the Enlightenment was instrumental in challenging common prejudices about old age, and supportive of older people's continued activity and participation in society. Troyanksy (1989: 217), writing about attitudes to old age in eighteenth-century France, suggests: 'A major movement of secularization downplayed the role of the afterlife, freeing old age from the hands of religion and death and permitting the elaboration of philosophical ideas for coping with longevity.' Although such trends were mostly beneficial to the middle and upper classes, the discrediting of beliefs about the evils of witchcraft had wider benefits – notably for older women who were a common target for accusations (Thomas, 1974).

McManners (1985: 84) examined attitudes towards death in eighteenth-century France, and argues that there was a psychological shift in views about ageing: 'Before they knew for sure that the pattern of mortality was improving, some of the affluent minority were abandoning fatalism about growing old and dying. Against logic, they wanted to live longer, and they were discovering the logic to insist on enjoying life and being useful at a greater age.' More optimistic views about longevity were, however, almost certainly confined to the middle classes, and it was well into the twentieth century before a 'belief in ageing' was likely to be encountered amongst working-class men and women. Nonetheless, in her research on attitudes towards ageing in eighteenth-century England, Ottaway (2004) identifies the emergence of old age as a distinct stage in life. Indeed, she even highlights some benefits to definitions of old age in this period:

> Because of a greater willingness to group the elderly into a chronologically defined set of people, local and national organizations (including the State) increasingly contemplated supplying monetary assistance to the aged. At the same time, because of the continuing fluidity of the definition of old age, people were never required to retire, enter a workhouse, or accept a pension merely because of their age. Thus there was not the kind of labelling of old people as necessarily impoverished, as was to happen in the twentieth century, with stereotypes about old-age pensioners. (2004: 64)

The eighteenth and nineteenth centuries saw the first attempts to describe and measure old age and ageing populations, notably through the activities of hospital doctors, statisticians and actuaries (Katz, 1996; von Kondratowitz, 2009). Chudacoff (1989: 53) suggests that by the 1890s the various ages of man were 'being defined with near-clinical precision, and more definite norms were being assigned to each stage'. This last point is crucial and reflects a major turning point in the social history of ageing. Prior to the nineteenth century it is clear that for all but the very rich, it was the challenges associated with poverty and chronic illness that marked old age – certainly there was no expectation of a settled period of life ahead of death. Surveying the period from the eleventh to the sixteenth century, Minois (1989: 306) concludes:

> The concept of retirement did not exist in any of these ancient periods, with the exception of a few privileged cases. Such distinctions as existed were between two categories of people: the active old, who in spite of their age, continued to exercise a profession and who merged into the mass of adult people as far as their contemporaries were concerned; and the inactive old, who were forced by their decrepitude to rest, and

were classed . . . among the infirm and the sick. There was thus no limit and old age disappeared . . . . In societies which were still very closed, where a person's status and membership of a group were the sole guarantors of social acceptance, where an isolated person could not survive, an old person was not recognized as such. So he had no rights and was entirely at the mercy of those around him. This was the social circle which, in the final analysis, created the image of old people, starting from the norms and human ideals of their age.

Thomas (1976: 248), commenting on the lives of older people in the sixteenth to the eighteenth century, summarizes the fate of most elderly people as follows:

For the old, wealth was frequently the only source of respect, once health and mind had started to decay. Given care, an elderly *rentier* could still retain his authority and be venerated for his wisdom and experience. But for those whose caring capacity depended on their physical strength, old age had little to commend it.

Financial support in old age

By the late nineteenth century, the outlines of a different kind of old age from that of previous centuries had begun to take shape, one which reflected the social and economic changes accompanying an industrialized and increasingly urbanized society. As Cole (1992: 114) notes: 'If medieval culture subordinated the ages of life to the pilgrimage of life in the interests of Christian eternity, Victorian culture reversed these priorities for the sake of productivity, progress and health.' The idea of a 'career' (with a pension at the end) was adopted in a number of professions. Civil servants had set an example with various pension systems already developed by the early nineteenth century (Hannah, 1986). Beyond the state sector, railway companies were important providers of pensions, although these invariably excluded manual or weekly paid employees. Amongst large employers in the new manufacturing industries, the development of occupational pensions was patchy, with a mixture of *ex gratia* payments as well as formal provision. The idea of a 'career' was, however, foreign to most working-class men and women, most of whom worked for as long as possible before disability or incapacity intervened. Very few would have had access to a pension, the exceptions being those in occupations such as mining and the railways (Stearns, 1975; Hannah, 1986).

On the one side, then, and especially before intervention from the state, pension provision in the late nineteenth and early twentieth centuries was limited to a select band of (mainly salaried) employees, notably civil servants, those working for the public utilities, and retired armed services officers. Hannah (1986: 13) calculates that, for the UK, '[i]t is unlikely that the number of employees in the *formally constituted* pension schemes in the public and private sectors combined exceeded a million even as late as 1900 . . . [covering] perhaps around 5% of the workforce'. Yet, on the other side, the idea of 'retirement' was increasingly encouraged by manufacturers, concerned with improving productivity in the workplace (Graebner, 1980). In the UK, the retirement of factory workers was assisted through workmen's compensation legislation, introduced in 1897. This required employers to insure against accidents at work and may have increased their tendency to discharge older and possibly accident-prone employees. According to Thane (1978: 236): 'Employers both introduced occupational pensions and pressed for a state scheme as this would let them lay-off older workers with clear consciences.' Fischer (1977), writing about old age in nineteenth-century America, suggests that the growth of the factory system accelerated the process of retirement, with the development of assembly-line methods hastening the discharge of older workers.

Technological change certainly created the right climate for retirement, but other factors were almost certainly involved. In the first place, older people probably entered the new industries at a slower rate than younger workers; equally, they tended to cluster in industries facing long-term decline. Second, retirement produced a number of benefits for industrial capitalism, notably in challenging security of tenure or 'jobs for life'. Third, as Graebner (1980) and Phillipson (1982) suggest, retirement played an important role in periods of mass unemployment, with the idea of older workers as surplus to labour requirements stimulating pension legislation in countries such as America, France and the UK.

The introduction of pensions provided by the state in a number of countries from the late nineteenth century was a tentative step towards acceptance of financial responsibility for a new period in the life course. The first state pensions were introduced in Germany in 1889, mainly for male workers aged 70, or an earlier age if they were permanently incapacitated. Britain introduced pensions from the age of 70 in 1908, reduced to 65 in 1925. Pension schemes followed much later in the case of Canada (in 1927) and the USA (in 1935 with the passing of the Social Security Act). In both cases benefits were made payable from the age of 70. Most of these schemes did little to help people made vulnerable through a combination of longevity and economic change. Few employees could continue working up to the age of 70 – especially those in working-class occupations. The (means-tested) five shillings (in the UK case) was around a fifth of the average wage and was clearly insufficient to compensate for lost earnings. In fact, as Hannah (1986: 16) notes, 'it was expressly presented as a supplement to support from casual earnings, charities, families, former employers, and the savings or friendly society benefits which the old were expected to accumulate'.

But the emerging outline of a pension system – state as well as occupational – is an important element in the modern story of ageing. It confirmed the basis of a new shape to the life course, with a separate phase distinct from that associated with employment. How to define this period of life, however, remained uncertain for some time. Society did become more aware of age and related demographic changes, but institutional responses remained hesitant at least up until the mid-twentieth century.

Becoming 'conscious of age'

For much of human history, age has carried a relatively limited set of meanings. As a social category, it had some influence on the individual's power and authority – although the intersection with class and gender has always been crucial (as continues to be the case). And age was certainly imbued with religious and spiritual significance in medieval times. But, as Chudacoff (1989: 9) observes, as a basis for categorizing people in society at large, age, from a historical perspective, held considerably less importance than it came to assume in the twentieth century. He suggests: '[K]nowing an individual's age did not automatically provide insight into that person's roles or social standing. Thus, age was more a biological phenomenon than a social attribute.' In the twentieth century this position was reversed and chronological age became closely tied to social norms and the allocation of resources of different kinds. Birthdays themselves (previously only celebrated by the better off) became important in marking transitions and 'rites of passage' through the life course (Chudacoff, 1989; Bytheway, 2009). Legal rights and duties became associated with particular ages, with access to a range of institutions moderated through age-based criteria. The various responsibilities associated with citizenship also became linked with age, including the right to vote, military service and duty to serve on a jury.

From the late nineteenth century, then, chronological age began to assume greater importance as a marker signifying progress through the life course. On the positive side, older people no longer 'disappeared' into the ranks of the poor, but were deemed worthy of specific support and assistance. On the negative side, emphasis on age as a social category became linked with specific attributes associated with chronological age, which were used to justify particular attitudes and practices towards older people. But reliance upon chronological age itself raises a number of difficulties. Baars (2009: 87), for example, observes: 'Persons are transformed into "aging", "aged" or "older" bodies at a particular chronological age without any evidence that important changes are taking place at that age apart from this sudden cultural relocation.' And Dannefer (2011: 4) makes the point: 'Despite extensive evidence that development and aging are contingent and modifiable processes, even social and behavioural scientists share the popular idea that many kinds of individual change "inevitably happen" with and are therefore "explained" by age.'

Baars (2012: 53) argues that our thinking about ageing has been overly dominated by chronometric ages, or clock time, to the extent that we tend to see a process of biological ageing running in synchrony with a clock that counts the years. He argues:

> Chronometric age is just a measurement of the time that has elapsed since someone was born. We are getting older with every tick of the clock, but this 'older' only has precise meaning in a chronometric not a gerontological sense. The 'aged' are extremely heterogeneous and have no more in common than a certain minimum calendar age. Dividing adults in age categories may seem practical but does not advance our understanding of ageing. Chronometric approaches are nevertheless quite dominant as age-related generalizations offer a superficial clarity that can be used to justify prejudice or systematic policies . . . If age-related generalizations are presented without further questioning their suggested meanings, there is a danger that conventional prejudices about ageing and the aged are reproduced or new ones introduced, even if the objective is to help and support [older people].

Yet the idea of 'variability' as the hallmark of late adult life has been resisted for much of the twentieth century. Our consciousness of 'age' – at least in relation to older people – has invariably focused upon their similarities as a group rather than their distinctiveness as individuals. From a sociological perspective, a number of reasons might be cited for this. In the first place, it is clear that many of the concepts which sociologists typically use in their work – such as class, gender and ethnicity – have often been applied sparingly in the case of elderly people. Yet, as suggested in the previous chapter, age may exacerbate rather than reduce inequalities experienced earlier in the life course. Social class remains, in many respects, a stronger predictor of lifestyle than age itself and older people are likely to have more in common with younger people of their own class than they will with older people from other social classes.

As well as social class, age is also affected by divisions associated with gender and ethnicity. The gender imbalances of later life are now well established. Because women (in many western societies) outlive men by an average of five years, there are around 50 per cent more women than men among those aged 65 and over. The gender imbalance is even more marked in late old age where, among those aged 85 and over, women outnumber men by three to one.

Race and ethnicity is another important division running through age-based relationships. The UK, as noted in Chapter 2, is now experiencing the ageing of the black and Asian communities, as cohorts of migrants from the 1950s onwards reach retirement and late old age. Older people from some minority ethnic groups are likely to have distinctive experiences in old age, including, first, increased susceptibility to physical ill-health because of past experiences such as heavy manual work and poor housing; second, great vulnerability to mental health problems – a product of racism and cultural pressures; third, acute financial problems, reflecting the cumulative disadvantages arising from low incomes and limited pensions. The problems faced by ethnic elders have been defined as a form of 'triple jeopardy' (Mutchler and Burr, 2011). This refers to the fact that ethnic elders face discrimination not only because they are old; in addition, many of them live in disadvantaged physical and economic circumstances; finally, they may also face discrimination because of their culture, language, skin colour or religious affiliation.

The above divisions have led one sociologist to conclude:

> People do not become more alike with age; in fact the opposite may well be the case . . .Their heterogeneity is entrenched in disparate master status characteristics, including membership groups and socio-economic circumstances, race, ethnicity, gender, sub-cultural, or structural conditions on the one hand, and personal attributes on the other. (Hendricks, 2003: 63; see also Formosa, 2009)

A second reason why 'age' seems to confer similarities may also be the legacy of poverty and dependency which has characterized the experience of growing old. Older people have always been a substantial group amongst those experiencing poverty. Indeed, in the UK, whether in the writings of Charles Dickens in the nineteenth century, surveys such as those by Rowntree in the 1930s, or the 're-discovery of poverty' in the 1960s (Townsend and Wedderburn, 1965; Coates and Silburn, 1970), older people figured prominently as a group experiencing long-term hardship. And even in the twenty-first century, despite improvements in their financial circumstances, we might still note the substantial proportion of older people living on incomes that fail to provide participation in society to any meaningful degree. In the UK, this affects around one in four single women aged 80-plus, one in five aged 60–69, and one in five men aged 80-plus (Jin et al., 2011; see also Chapter 6). Yet, despite the case that these experiences have mostly been class- and gender-related, age has always been produced as a more important 'explanation', as if there are some 'natural properties' attached to growing old which draw people into poverty. This may have been – and continues to be – a convenient explanation for societies that fail to provide adequate resources for people to live without too much hardship. Problems attributed to 'age' seem to take responsibility away from the institutional forces that produce the condition in the first place. They also help to 'objectify' older people as a group with more experiences in common than ones which divide, a viewpoint which even sociologists have found hard to resist.

Conclusion

This chapter has examined the gradual emergence of old age as a distinct stage in life, taking shape first among the wealthy and middle classes but influencing as well (albeit introducing new insecurities) the lives of working-class men and women. As will be argued in more detail in the following chapter, chronological age, with its emphasis on similarities rather than differences, became more important in the twentieth century with the institutionalization of the life course and rites of passage linked with schooling, employment and retirement. These institutions, along with the introduction of the welfare state, created a powerful set of arrangements which served to define the social status of older people. The development of an 'orderly and calculable' set of phases through life seemed to offer the solution to the structural and biographical challenges posed by ageing societies (Kohli, 1986: 287). The idea of a 'predictable' phase in life which could be planned in advance promised significant gains over the insecurities which had been the lot of older people in past societies. Yet the disadvantages of this approach, as will be explored in further chapters, soon became apparent: first, in the way that major differences among older people were ignored; second, in the way that the basis on which an 'orderly life course' could be delivered were themselves unstable. Indeed, it is clear that this kind of approach assumed a degree of economic stability which was only available for a relatively short period of time. Thereafter, what counted as 'old' and the nature of ageing itself came up for fresh evaluation.

5

The Social Construction of Ageing

Introduction

In the twentieth century, western society developed various forms of support linked with social classifications based around age. These emerged through the extension of dependency at the beginning of the life course, initially associated with secondary education and, subsequently, with the expansion of higher education. Following this came paid employment and unpaid caring, occupying a span of chronological ages from the twenties to the sixties. This was a period (at least for men in middle-class occupations and those from 'elite' working groups) defined in terms of 'stable careers' built around the accumulation of rights to a pension (typically of a 'defined benefit' type) complementing that provided by the state. Thereafter, increasingly at ages 60 (for women) and 65 (for men) the idea of 'retirement' from work took hold, with a new phase in life defined, initially, as a time of 'rest' ('dependency' according to some interpretations), subsequently a 'third age' of active involvement in community life.

However, almost as soon as these developments took hold – mainly over the course of the 1970s and 1980s – the economic conditions underpinning the new life course disintegrated. Older people were, once again, forced onto the defensive, with ideological, financial and social challenges arising from conditions of economic austerity. This chapter reviews this transformation in the experience of ageing from the mid-twentieth century towards the new crisis of legitimacy affecting institutions supporting older people in the opening two decades of the twenty-first. Approaches to social ageing shifted dramatically over this period, and with this the social status and financial position of different groups of older people. This chapter assesses the changes involved in the key institutions supporting elderly people.

Transforming old age: The emergence of retirement and the welfare state

As a starting point, it is important to emphasize the way in which old age was transformed in the two decades following the ending of the Second World War. The key development here concerned the way in which, in advanced capitalist countries, growing old was reconstructed through the social and economic institutions linked with mandatory retirement and the welfare state. These became crucial in shaping the dominant discourse around which ageing was framed, and the identities with which it was associated. A supporting theme was the reordering of the life course into distinctive stages (or 'boxes' as they came to be termed – see Best, 1980) associated with education, work and retirement, with the transition between the last two becoming an important element in the fashioning of a new identity separate from that associated with work and paid employment (Phillipson, 2002; Grenier, 2012).

This new life course was underpinned by the development of the welfare state with newly established health and social services for older people. Debates in the 1940s and early 1950s had highlighted the need to escape the injustices and deprivation experienced during the depression of the 1930s (Hennessy, 1993). Following this, Lowe (1993: 21) views the creation of the welfare state as an attempt to move society to a 'higher ethical ground', 'institutionalising a deeper sense of community and mutual care'. In Britain, welfare for older people was defined in three main ways from the 1950s to the 1970s. Pensions were the first and overriding concern, an issue which 'dominated the agenda as much as relief payments had done in an earlier era' (Parker, 1990: 8). Next was the focus on residential and institutional care (a feature of the 1948 National Assistance Act). Then there was the continuing role of the voluntary sector (under the aegis of bodies such as the National Old People's Welfare Council) in providing a range of limited domiciliary provision within the community (Roberts, 1970). Of continued importance, however, was the role of the family in providing essential support to older people (illustrated in landmark studies by Sheldon [1948] and Townsend [1957]). In this context, the early postwar period created one welfare state (largely focused on pensions and residential care), but kept in place the existing 'welfare state' built around the families of older people. These two 'pillars', along with support from the voluntary sector, represented the form in which old age was constructed as a welfare issue and problem.

It is, of course, possible to exaggerate the impact of the welfare state on the lives of older people. Beveridge's (1942) strictures about avoiding the 'extravagance [of] giving a full subsistence income to every citizen, as a birthday present on his or her reaching the age of 60 or 65', were taken to heart by most governments over succeeding decades. The flat-rate pension introduced in 1948 was more generous than previous arrangements but allowed for a very modest standard of living. As Thane (2000: 367) notes: '[The state pension] was designed to relieve poverty rather than, like . . . systems emerging in most other west European countries, to provide in old age an income related to income during working life . . . preventing a catastrophic decline when paid work ceased.'

The legacy of poor law provision for the old could still be found in warehouse-like residential and long-stay homes, as described by Peter Townsend in *The Last Refuge* (1962) and by Barbara Robb and her colleagues in *Sans Everything* (1967), a study of older people in 'mental hospitals'. Kynaston (2009: 631), in his survey of Britain in the 1950s, suggests: 'It seems to have been axiomatic among hospital administrators and health authorities that geriatric patients, being "chronic", only merited a lower budget, including for food, than acute patients.' (Chapter 8 provides a review of continuing problems in the area.) Jack Shaw (1971) exposed the squalid conditions of those living in the community in his powerful study of elderly people in Sheffield. Older people were the largest single group 'rediscovered' as living in poverty in the early 1960s, although governments (abetted by civil servants) were in denial for some time that this could possibly be the case (Townsend and Wedderburn, 1965; see also Coates and Silburn, 1970).

However, the possibility of transforming old age, through improvements to income, health and social care, was a significant feature of discussions in the 1940s and 1950s. Care for older people was viewed both as a fair exchange for past work and services (with the sacrifices of war still a vital part of folk memory) and as a way of resolving some of the insecurities and undoubted suffering associated with the final phase of the life course (Judt, 2005). But if the welfare state created – or set out to create – a new basis for old age, it was the transformation in welfare from the 1970s and 1980s onwards which posed a fresh challenge to the status and identity of older people. The crisis in ageing that took hold from this period largely reflected the loosening of the institutional supports underpinning the life course.

The emergence of retirement

Older people – as a social category – can themselves be viewed as a creation of modernity reflecting the achievements of industrialization, improved public health and the growth of social welfare (Achenbaum, 2010; Thane, 2000). For a period from 1950 to 1970, moving older people into those institutions associated with retirement and the welfare state appeared to have resolved the issue of achieving security. The meaning of later life was, temporarily at least, developed through a vision whereby retirement and welfare were viewed as natural supports to the end of the human life cycle. The idea of 'retirement' was an essential part of the narrative driving the reconstruction of ageing. In the 1950s and 1960s, retirement at age 60 (in the case of women) and 65 (in the case of men) became widely established. Indeed, '[b]y the late 1960s it was accepted that the *normal* period of full-time employment would cease for *most* of the population at these ages' (Harper and Thane, 1989: 59). Retirement thus became an important 'social institution' regulating the passage from work to the final stages of the life course (Kohli, 1986).

This movement of people out of the workplace – at a point marked by the drawing of state pensions – was further reinforced by the availability of occupational pensions for (mainly) men from middle-class and a limited number of skilled working-class occupations. Growth in membership of private sector schemes (along with the steady expansion of the public sector) had been substantial in the boom years of the 1950s and 1960s. The total number of occupational scheme members increased from 8 million in 1956 (around one-third of the work force) to 12.2 million in 1967 (almost one-half of the workforce) (Hannah, 1986).

The pattern set in the 1950s and 1960s was for most men to remain in work up until the age of 65, but for a minority to stay on for varying lengths of time after their 65th birthday. In 1961, 91 per cent of men aged 60–64 were in work or looking for work; this dropped to 25 per cent for those aged 65-plus. The pattern begins to change, however, from the mid-1960s, driven by the contraction of key areas of manufacturing along with rising levels of unemployment (Dex and Phillipson, 1986). By 1971, 83 per cent of men aged 60–64 were in employment, compared with 19 per cent of those aged 65-plus; by 1981, the equivalent figures had fallen to 69 per cent and 10 per cent. By 1991, the number in or looking for work among men aged 60–64 had fallen again, to 54 per cent, and remained at 10 per cent of those aged 65-plus. Put another way, while in 1950 the average age of exit from employment (for men) was 67.2 years, with life expectancy at age of exit from the workforce of 10.8 years, by 2000 the equivalent figures were 63.3 and 19.8 years. This meant – expressed as a percentage of time adults spent in retirement – an increase from 18% in 1950 to 30% in 2000 (Pensions Commission, 2004).

From a sociological perspective two contrasting features emerged in the late 1960s and the 1970s regarding the experience of work in middle and later life. First, leaving employment came to be viewed (for men at least) as part of a 'mass transition', with associated 'rites of passage' (Crawford, 1971). Linked to this comes a discussion about the value of retirement as a 'distinctive' phase in life, together with the importance of 'preparation' and 'planning' (Help the Aged, 1979; Phillipson, 1981) and the case for developing a 'third age' built around securing 'personal achievements' separate from those associated with work (Laslett, 1989).

However, almost as soon as the outlines of a settled period had appeared, it became clear that long-term changes affecting the working life were creating instabilities for retirement itself. Researchers began to draw a distinction between 'retirement', on the one side, and 'early exit', on the other. The former refers to entry into a public-provided old-age pension scheme; the latter, early withdrawal from paid employment supported through unemployment, disability or associated benefits (Kohli et al., 1991). Rather than employment ending after a set number of years and at a fixed chronological age, there was now a measure of ambiguity about when the working life ended and retirement began. The previous template of a long working life followed by a short retirement was being eroded: for a majority of workers through greater insecurity in the workplace; for a minority through the attractiveness of retirement given the safety net of an occupational pension (Schuller, 1989).

Martin Kohli (1986) and Anne-Marie Guillemard (1989) came to view these changes as part of the 'de-standardization of the life course'. They argued that evidence that people were withdrawing from work at earlier ages suggested the 'break-up' of the type of retirement that had emerged across most western industrial countries in the 1950s and 1960s. The chronological milestones which once marked the life course had become invisible, while the time for withdrawal from work was no longer fixed at a predictable point. In this new world, Guillemard argued:

> There is less and less of a definite order to the last phase in life. The life course is being de-institutionalized. Along with the abandonment of conventional retirement, we also see the break-up of ... the threefold model which placed the

individual in a foreseeable life course of continuous, consecu-
tive sequences of functions and statuses. As a consequence,
an individual's working life now ends in confusion. (1989:
177).

These arguments suggested a new form of crisis in the lives
of older people, reflecting the restructuring of work in the
1970s and 1980s – now linked with global economic changes
– along with the challenge to traditional assumptions about
the nature of the life course. What seemed to have 'come
apart' (to use Guillemard's phrase) was the notion of a stable
period of retirement, built upon an orderly phase of work
and occupation. Work itself became less stable in this period,
with the rise of 'flexible' employment, short-term contracts
and the downsizing of industries (Sennett, 1998). For older
workers, the significance of economic decline was reinforced
by a demographic context whereby a substantial cohort of
younger people was now entering the labour market. Older
workers became targeted as a key group to be removed from
employment, reflected in the terminology of the period – i.e.
'redundancies', shake-outs' and 'early retirement'.

Views about the *benefits* of retirement also began to feature
more prominently from the 1970s. Cribier (1981) demonstrated a change among French retirees interviewed during
this period. The younger cohorts in her study demonstrated
an increase in the proportion of people who viewed retirement as a desirable goal, with early retirement seen as especially attractive. This research reflected findings in the US
(Atchley, 1971) and in the UK (Phillipson, 1993). For a
period, this 'de-standardization' of the life course seemed to
offer new possibilities for a 'liberated retirement', with the
idea of the 'third age' explored in a variety of ways through
the 1980s and 1990s (Laslett, 1989; Gilleard and Higgs,
2000). However, this change to the life course had two major
requirements if more ambitious lifestyles were to be realized:
first, that the idea of an 'active retirement' was accepted as a
legitimate stage of the life course; second, that sufficient
resources should be provided through the different income
'pillars' associated with the welfare state, employers and personal savings. Both these aspects were, however, to unravel
over the course of the 1990s and 2000s, with dramatic

reversals in the fortunes of older people themselves (see further Chapter 6).

Destabilizing ageing and retirement

Support for retirement as a major stage in the life course came under pressure from the mid-1990s, with debates moving back to emphasizing the importance of older people retaining an attachment to work and the 'unaffordable' nature of retirement in its traditional form (Liedtke and Schanz, 2012). With the move out of economic recession, attempts were made to reverse the pattern of early exit and early retirement from work. Governments across most industrial countries became concerned about the economic consequences of ageing populations and the associated costs of pensions and care services (Organisation for Economic Co-operation and Development, 2006). The age at which people could gain access to state pensions was raised in many countries alongside measures to tackle age discrimination in the workplace.

The impact of the above measures was, however, mixed. In the UK, the employment rate of men aged 60–64 remained unchanged at around 50–55 per cent over the period from 1991 to 2011 (i.e., even covering the period of economic growth in the late 1990s and early 2000s). The rate for men aged 65–69 did increase from 18 per cent to around 24 per cent over the course of the 2000s (related in part to financial difficulties facing those whose occupational pensions provided less than they were expecting to receive). The average age of withdrawal from the labour market also increased, from 63.8 years in 2004 to 64.6 in 2010 (Office for National Statistics [ONS], 2012c). Among women, there was a substantial increase in employment among those aged 60–64, moving from 24.1 in 1991 to 33.9 in 2010; for those aged 65–69 there was a rise from 3 per cent in 1991 to 16.2 per cent in 2011 (the majority of women in both age groups employed in part-time positions). The average age of withdrawal from the labour market for women increased from 61.2 years in 2004 to 64.6 years in 2010 (ONS, 2012c).

At the same time, it is clear that the swing back to encouraging older people to remain in work raises a number of issues regarding support for older people in general. Ambiguity remains in terms of how work ends. Indeed, a slight majority of men and women in the UK still leave employment ahead of their 65th birthday (one-quarter of men are out of the workforce before the age of 59). Against this, mechanisms to encourage people back into work appear limited. In the UK, the evidence is that, once out of employment, compared with other age groups, those aged 50 and over find it harder to get back into work. The proportion of the older group unemployed for over a year has risen from 33 per cent (in 2008) to 44.5 per cent (in 2012). Older workers have also seen the biggest increases in redundancies over the course of the recession (Cory, 2012). Discrimination against older workers appears to have increased during a period of economic recession. Research in the US shows that age discrimination complaints with the Federal Employment Opportunity Commission were up 29 per cent in 2008, compared with 2007 (cited in Ekerdt, 2010). In the current decade, there are likely to be continuing pressures to extend the working life, but with 'exclusionary' forces, especially from employers under pressure to reduce costs in the workplace. The impact of large-scale unemployment, in high- as well as low-income countries, will almost certainly create severe restrictions on the opportunities available to older employees.

On the other side, the ability of people to finance their retirement (see further Chapter 7) appears to have become more restricted, with the economic recession accelerating changes in financial and pension arrangements. The containment of ageing within the institutions of retirement and the welfare state was finally dissolved following the banking collapse of 2008. The impact of this was immediate in terms of financial provision in old age. In the UK, the onset of recession led to a sharp drop in contributions to personal and stakeholder pensions – a 10 per cent reduction over the period 2008–10 (ONS, 2011c). The collapse in share prices caused pension pots to shrink from £552 billion to £391 billion over a 17-month period from October 2007. Research has suggested declines in the median income of pensioners in the order of 2.4 per cent over the period 2008/9–2011/12, with low interest rates on savings a key factor. This reduction compared with falls of 1.1 per cent for working-age households with children and 1.8 per cent for those without (Browne, 2011). In the US, Burtless (2009: 73) highlighted the way falling asset prices resulting from stock market fluctuations affected retirement incomes:

> Between October 31st 2007 and October 31st 2008 stock market prices in the US fell 37.5 per cent. Because consumer prices rose nearly 5 per cent during the same period, newly retired workers who had invested nearly all their savings in the US stock market saw the purchasing power of their nest eggs shrink by more than 40 per cent.

Reflecting the above changes, and even before the economic crisis of 2008, researchers had begun to identify retirement as involving new risks and insecurities. On the one side, retirement appeared to have been 'reinvented as a time of transition to a new life, rather than simply an old one' (Hockey and James, 2003: 102). On the other, this 'new life' began to take on many trappings of the old one in respect of a deepening of social and economic inequalities (Vickerstaff and Cox, 2005). The next section reviews the new 'individualization' of retirement, linked initially with the rise of the 'risk society' but reinforced though political globalization and, subsequently, economic recession.

From welfare state to risk society

From the 1990s onwards, the crisis affecting retirement and the welfare state illustrated the way social marginality among the old had been contained rather than resolved. Moreover, what a postmodern society did have to offer – the shift in emphasis from production to consumption – seemed only to create further difficulties for those living on the economic margins. Bauman, for example, writes of the accelerating emancipation of capital from labour producing a situation where, 'instead of engaging the rest of society in the role of producers, capital tends to engage them in the role of consumers' (1992: 111). This transformation in fact reflected a more general shift from the public provision characteristic of what Lash and Urry (1987) refer to as 'organized capitalism', to the more flexible arrangements running through the period of 'disorganized capitalism'.

This development was to challenge definitions of what it meant to be an 'older person' and associated ideologies of support. The focus on growing old moved from collective responsibilities towards an emphasis on the way in which families and individuals should handle the demands associated with longevity. This new development may be seen as characteristic of a society where the 'social production of risk' runs alongside that associated with the 'social production of wealth' (Beck, 1992). Improved life expectancy, as already noted, may itself be viewed as a consequence of the social transformations associated with modernization. Beck (1992: 21) defines the nature of risk as a *'systematic way of dealing with hazards and insecurities induced and introduced by modernization itself'* (emphasis in original). Of course, older people have been ever present in human history, and often in positions that emphasize their relative powerlessness when faced with poverty, bereavement and ill-health. But to paraphrase Beck, in the past these could be seen as personal rather than societal tragedies. The impact of older people was restricted by the relatively superficial nature of the category of 'pensioner' or 'elderly person' and by their limited demographic profile. Changes accompanying modernization have transformed both these elements, with ageing becoming a new and socially recognized risk.

However, in line with Beck's thesis about the nature of risk society, three characteristics have become apparent with the maturation of ageing populations. First, the 'global' dimensions to ageing are (as observed in Chapter 2) increasingly important (Higo and Williamson, 2011). All societies (poor as well as rich) experience growth both in the numbers and proportions of older people in their populations. Ageing thus becomes simultaneously both an individual event and one shared with different cultures and societies across the globe. Second, ageing populations take on increasing diversity in respect of incomes and lifestyles, reflecting contrasting experiences both between and within birth cohorts. Third, older people both transform and are transformed by social and economic institutions. Again, Beck (1992: 10) captures this dimension when he argues that 'the more societies are modernized the more agents (subjects) acquire the ability to reflect upon the social conditions of their existence and to change them in that way'. For older people, this raised the possibility of moving from conditions of dependency towards consumer-based lifestyles (Gilleard and Higgs, 2005). Against this, Vickerstaff and Cox (2005: 92) suggest that the result of what they term the 'individualization of retirement' has been 'less to increase the majority of people's range of alternatives and choices over when and how to retire and more to enlarge the range of risks they [have] to cope with'.

Redefining later life

From a sociological perspective, the changes reviewed in this chapter have transformed the way in which old age is experienced and located within the life course. The shift has been from the stages of life characteristic of pre- and early modern times and the 'three boxes' of education, work and retirement characteristic of the mid- to late twentieth century, towards a more fluid and unstable landscape surrounding the latter end of the life course. Polivka (2000) views this development as reflecting the increasingly 'improvizational' nature of the life course, with people cultivating the capacity to adjust to discontinuity in key areas of their life. Such changes raise questions about the way in which social ageing is evolving, given the restructuring of retirement and the welfare state. Settersten and Trauten suggest that, for older people, the future seems open but also fragile. They observe:

> Choices now seem greater, but these choices seem heavier and come with unknown consequences. Any fall-outs must be negotiated and absorbed by individuals and their families rather than by governments, markets, or other entities . . . [T] he trend towards individualization means that old people are increasingly left to their own devices to determine the directions that the ends of their lives will take. Old people are largely on their own with only the safety nets they can create with the resources they have, whether through personal and

family resources or through social skills and psychological capacities. (2009: 457)

The unravelling of traditional institutions has exposed once again the cultural uncertainties surrounding old age (Cole, 1992). Western society is beset, as during the 1930s and 1940s, with anxieties about the most appropriate way to respond to an ageing population. Particular groups (notably the baby boom generation) have been singled out as causing particular problems – creating tensions between generations and drawing down a disproportionate share of economic resources. Willetts (2010: xxi) summarizes the issues as follows:

> At the moment this [baby boom] generation dominates just about every important institution in the country: it has most of the wealth and power. How will this generation discharge its obligations to younger generations? So far it has been one of the luckiest generations. Will the boomers be selfish with their luck, or will they pass it on to the next generation? So far the evidence is not good. The baby boomers, having enjoyed so far a spectacularly good deal, are dumping too many problems on the younger generation. It has the great advantage of being a giant generation but how will it use that power? At the moment it looks like a selfish giant.

There are a number of problems with this type of argument: the UK baby boom could never be described as a 'giant generation' in the way that might in some respects be accurate for countries such as Australia and the US. Unlike the latter two, the UK did not experience a sustained baby boom from the mid-1940s through to the mid-1960s. Rather, there were two separate 'spikes' – in the late 1940s to the early 1950s (best termed – as it was at the time - a 'bulge' rather than a 'boom') – and then another in the early 1960s. Birth cohorts (a more accurate term than 'generations') do not tend to behave either in 'selfish' or 'altruistic' ways; instead, political action is generally fragmented by the usual markers of class, gender and ethnicity. And certainly not all baby boomers have enjoyed a 'spectacularly good deal', especially (as we shall see in Chapter 7) in terms of access to resources for old age. Inequalities among those approaching retirement were illustrated in the *Anatomy of Economy Inequality* produced by Hills et al. (2010). This demonstrated that for individuals aged between 55 and 64 in England and Wales, the top income decile of managerial and professionals have more than £2.1 million in household wealth, compared to the less than £13,000 owned by the bottom income decile in routine/ semi-routine occupations) (Hills et al., 2010).

But the accuracy of arguments about baby boomers is probably less important than the view that a particular group is about to reap 'undeserved' benefits in old age. Underlying this appears to be a suggestion that support provided by the welfare state is likely to switch from the poor and the young to the old and the rich. Concerns about the costs of support for old people are not, as noted elsewhere in this book, themselves new. They had a relatively low profile in the 1950s and 1960s in the context of full employment and the building of the welfare state (Kynaston, 2009). They surfaced in the late 1970s in the context of economic crisis and the rise of neo-liberal governments, with emphasis placed on the pressure on working family budgets from pension contributions and related benefits (Longman, 1987). And they returned with particular vigour in the 2000s, when the coincidence of economic recession and the movement of baby boomers into retirement drew attention to lifestyles which had seemingly caused the crisis and which, at the same time, would bring considerable problems in the years ahead (Howker and Malik, 2010). These shifts in perceptions about ageing populations reflect continuing fragility in how ageing – and old age in particular - is constructed across the life course. In this context, the twenty-first century has reopened rather than resolved the place and status of older people in society.

Conclusion

Ageing populations do, it would follow from the above, bring to the surface wider anxieties about the direction of social change. In line with this, Cole (1992: 235), summarizing concerns expressed in the late 1980s in America, argued:

[O]ld age has again emerged as a lightning rod for the storms of liberal capitalism and middle-class identity. This time, it is the middle-aged baby boomers who are most susceptible to neoconservative Cassandras who forecast Armaggedon and the bankruptcy of . . . government. Fears about declining fertility and the burden of an ageing population merge with the fiscal and ideological crisis of the welfare state. Personal anxieties about growing old are conflated with pessimism about the future. Critics and commentators represent the aging of our social institutions with metaphors of decline, exhaustion and collapse. Our ageing society does indeed bring with it unprecedented problems but the spectre of old age obscures its possibilities.

Cole (1992) develops the argument that, in emphasizing the problems attached to ageing populations, we were in danger of ignoring the undoubted successes and possibilities they might be said to represent. The former were illustrated in Chapter 2, where the dramatic and continued growth in life expectancy was highlighted. The latter is reflected in the development of policies such as those associated with 'active ageing' (European Commission, 1999), with the involvement of older people in numerous activities sustaining their families and communities – thus ensuring 'reciprocity' rather than 'conflicts' between generations. Against this, the force of Riley and Riley's (1994) 'structural lag hypothesis' continues to be apparent, with the argument that social institutional structures lag behind the years of extra life, resulting in diminished opportunities for engagement in social roles and activities. In the nineteenth century and for much of the twentieth, ageing seemed to have been secured in the context of a life course which promised a stable career followed by an equally stable period of retirement. Yet the institution of retirement was never completely accepted. Preparation for retirement emerged for a period (mainly in the 1960s and 1970s) but covered only a fraction of the workforce (Phillipson, 1981). Much of the literature on retirement was keen to stress its negative impact on people apparently unused to large chunks of leisure. Although evidence for this was effectively undermined by longitudinal studies in the 1970s and 1980s (Phillipson, 1993), pressure to bring people back into work from the 1990s onwards again raised question-marks over the legitimacy of people leaving work in their fifties and sixties (despite them being urged to do so just a decade earlier).

Reflecting on the above, what seemed to come apart in the 1990s was 'any agreed language of retirement, that is categories, concepts and the links between them that people can access to describe and situate their own experience' (Vickerstaff and Cox, 2005: 91). Yet if the 'language of retirement' had failed, that regarding 'old age' was even more disputed, both by those concerned with its potential economic costs (see above and Chapter 2) and by those feeling vulnerable to the stigma the label seemed to impose on them. In many ways, albeit for different reasons, age and old age seemed to be as uncertain in their direction in the twenty-first century as they had been in previous centuries. Over the past decade this has been massively reinforced by the crisis affecting various elements in the institutions supporting older people. Part II explores the construction of ageing in more detail through the areas of pensions, family life and health and social care provision in late old age.

Part II
Inequalities and Divisions in Later Life

6

Ageing and Pensions: The Social Construction of Inequality

Introduction

A major goal for social policy, in all industrialized countries, has been to secure income security for older people. Initially, the focus was on tackling extreme poverty and destitution – especially among those in late old age. Gradually, aspirations shifted towards achieving replacement of pre- to post-working incomes at a level which would allow continuity of lifestyles from work to retirement. Countries, as noted in Chapter 4, have diverged considerably in terms of the development of pension support. Europe introduced embryonic national insurance and pension schemes from the late nineteenth century onwards. The US created its own national retirement programme in 1935 with the passing of the Social Security Act. In the UK, the 1942 Beveridge Report laid the basis for legislation on social insurance passed in 1948. In general, though, at least up until the early 1950s, support for older people in most western countries remained extremely modest, reflecting legislation built around the language of 'poor relief' as opposed to that of 'social insurance' (Blackburn, 2002).

The purpose of this chapter is to examine issues relating to inequality in late life with specific reference to pension provision, taking Britain as an example, but with reference to the US and other countries for comparison. The argument put forward is that the changes outlined in previous chapters are most clearly illustrated in the field of pensions, and the associated 'individualization of risk'. However, the topics discussed, although technical in part, do highlight central issues in the way ageing is being constructed in the twenty-first century, notably the extent to which financial arrangements that support people through the life course encourage or undermine beliefs about the reality of ageing. The theoretical framework adopted draws upon that of critical gerontology, exploring the role of pensions in constructing experiences of dependency and exclusion in old age (Estes, 1979; Walker and Foster, 2006). To develop a critical analysis of contemporary issues around pensions, this chapter will, first, sketch the evolution of pensions in industrial countries over the post-war period; second, summarize the impact of neo-liberal social policies from the late 1970s onwards and the new context of economic globalization; third, review the pensions crisis arising from the individualization of risk and welfare; finally, indicate new areas that are emerging which influence issues relating to pensions and inequality.

Post-war developments in pensions

Public provision for pensions has been a contested area within social policy. Up until the 1950s, public pension schemes in most industrialized countries tended to be modest in scope, both in the amount of money provided and in respect of the groups covered within the working population. In the majority of cases, replacement rates barely reached 20 per cent of the average wage (13 per cent in the UK in 1939; 17 per cent in Canada; 21 per cent in the US). The level of support itself reflected the underlying goal of public sector schemes – namely, that of providing bare subsistence and reducing the overall level of poverty (World Bank, 1994).

The period from the early 1950s through to the mid-1970s was, if not exactly a 'golden age' for retirees (Hannah, 1986), certainly one of progress in respect of the development of pensions. The rapid expansion of occupational (employer-based) schemes was one element (see also Chapter 5). In the

UK, employers used pensions (especially in the 1950s and 1960s) to cultivate a loyal workforce in a context of widespread shortages of skilled labour (Phillipson, 1982). Whiteside (2006) notes how some European countries, faced with the social and economic devastation arising from the Second World War, introduced citizenship pensions (illustrated by Sweden and the Netherlands) to prevent destitution in old age. In the US, economic prosperity fostered the expansion of employer-based pensions, but with labour unions such as the United Mine Workers also influencing the adoption of pensions as a key item in collective bargaining (Sass, 1989).

In the case of the UK, post-Second World War government policy increasingly emphasized the need for public provision to be supplemented by other forms of support. Pemberton et al. (2006) see this as integral to a view of state pensions as playing a residual role in comparison with commercial providers, personal savings or employment. In reality, this was always going to penalize substantial groups in the population, notably those in poorly paid employment, those engaged in full-time personal care, the self-employed and those in unstable employment. Little wonder that after the burst of optimism about social reform was over, it was the poverty of older people that was thrust into the limelight, with studies in the UK such as *The Poor and the Poorest* (Abel-Smith and Townsend, 1965) and in the US *The Other America* (Harrington, 1963) highlighting the scale of financial problems facing elderly people.

Pensions also became associated, from the 1950s onwards, with the 'social creation of dependency', the result of mandatory retirement imposed on people simply by virtue of reaching a certain age (Walker, 1980; Townsend, 1981). Income from employment gradually reduced in importance for older people through the 1950s and 1960s; indeed, with the spread of earlier retirement from the 1970s, the period spent outside the labour market was substantially increased. At the same time, public pensions – in most countries – continued to be set below (substantially so in many cases) average earnings. In the UK, occupational pension provision saw a marked increase in the number of active members between 1953 and 1967 – from 6.2 million to 12.2 million – but with most schemes providing relatively small amounts and with significant groups such as blue-collar workers and women excluded from membership.[1]

Any gains in pension provision were subsequently challenged by the neo-liberal agenda influencing social policy from the late 1970s. In the 1950s, as Johnson and Falkingham (1992) observe, the move to an unfunded pay-as-you-go (PAYG) system (i.e., one paid directly from current workers' contributions and taxes) slipped through without controversy. Economic growth provided a sense that state support for pensions could be guaranteed so long as income and expenditure were kept roughly in balance each year. The 1970s, however, brought early questioning of the PAYG system, as social security now came to be viewed as an obstacle rather than an aid to economic efficiency. Increased expenditure on pensions placed them under the spotlight in debates about the future of the welfare state (Myles, 1984). In the UK, plans for pension reform and for strengthening the public sector were abandoned in the 1980s, to be replaced by a weakened state pension system, an extension of means testing and accelerated pension privatization (Walker, 1991).

In a climate stressing the economic threat associated with demographic ageing as well as the possibility of conflict between workers and pensioners over resources (Johnson et al., 1989), the desirability of limiting reliance on PAYG systems became a central theme in debates (Vincent, 2003). This was reinforced with the publication by the World Bank (1994: 21) of *Averting the Old Age Crisis*, which set out the case for moving away from what was viewed as an 'ever more costly public pillar', underpinned by 'high tax rates that inhibit growth and bring low rates of return to workers'. Apart from recommendations to increase the retirement age, limit rewards for early retirement and downsize benefit levels (reforms which were already under way in many countries), the World Bank advocated the launch of a 'second [private] pillar with appropriate contribution and regulatory structures' (1994: 22). The benefits of this were seen in terms of increasing long-term saving, developing fully funded pensions and diversifying risk through a mix of public and private management.

Through the 1990s and into the 2000s, benefits linked to public pension systems went into decline. PAYG remained in place in maturing pension systems, but the ages at which benefits could be drawn were usually increased, together with modifications to the contribution periods required. At the same time, a development in many countries was the move away from defined benefit (DB) schemes in favour of the 'portability' associated with defined contribution (DC) schemes, which placed the burden of risk and decision-making onto the shoulders of the individual worker (see further below).

Globalization and pension reform

The drive towards pension reform has been given further impetus by the trends associated with globalization. A key dimension in this regard has been the way in which inter-governmental organizations (IGOs) have contributed to what has been termed the 'crisis construction and crisis management' of policies for older people (Estes and Associates, 2001). Deacon (2000) suggests that globalization generates a global discourse within and among global actors on the future of social policy, with pension provision a major area of attention. Yeates (2001: 122) observes: 'Both the World Bank and IMF have been at the forefront of attempts to foster a political climate conducive to [limiting the scope of] state welfare . . . and the promotion [instead] of . . . private and voluntary initiatives.' This position has influenced both national governments and transnational bodies such as the International Labour Organization (ILO) and the Organisation for Economic Co-operation and Development (OECD), with an emerging consensus around support for minimal public pension provision, an extended role for individualized and capitalized private pensions, and the raising of the retirement age.

This debate produced a significant discussion about pension provision and retirement ages, but it has largely excluded perspectives which might suggest an enlarged role for the state, and those which might question the stability and cost-effectiveness of private schemes. The ILO concluded early in the debate: 'Investing in financial markets is an uncertain and volatile business: under present pension plans people may save up to 30 per cent more than they need – which would reduce their spending during their working life; or they may save 30 per cent too little – which would severely cut their spending in retirement' (Gillion et al., 2000). Add in as well the crippling administrative charges associated with the running of private schemes, and the advocacy of market-based provision hardly seems as persuasive as most IGOs have been keen to present (Blackburn, 2006).

Globalization gave impetus to a new conception of managing social ageing, one based around what Ferge (1997b) referred to as the 'individualization of the social'. The language of social insurance was gradually displaced by the 'personalization' or 'individualization' of risk. Dannefer (2000: 270) summarizes this process in the following way: '[C]orporate and state uncertainties are transferred to citizens – protecting large institutions while exposing individuals to possible catastrophe in the domains of health and personal care finances, justified to the public by the claim that the pensioner can do better on his or her own.'

What evidence is there, however, that the individual pensioner is doing 'better'? What has been the record since the process of pension reform started back in the 1980s? Has the aspiration of the World Bank for more efficient and equitable pensions been achieved? The next section of this chapter examines the record to date, with a focus on evidence from the UK but with reference as well to other countries.

Privatizing pensions: The management of risk

The area of pensions is invariably viewed as one of the most complex aspects of social policy. This is certainly the case for those working within the discipline. It is even more the case for those either contributing to or receiving a pension. Cowling (2010: 15) observes: 'The UK has the most complicated pension system in the world. The second tier of State pensions is so complicated that few have any idea what their [pension] is likely to be which makes planning for retirement very difficult.' At the same time, increasing numbers of people pay into a defined contribution pension fund, managed on their behalf. Those contributing, however, will have minimal involvement or understanding about investment decisions which are likely to determine their living standards for around one-third of their life (Harrison, 2012; see further below).

The argument of this chapter is that problems in relation to pensions have become increasingly influential in shaping attitudes towards ageing. The extent to which people have confidence about planning the direction of their lives, especially as they enter their 50s and 60s, is geared around the resources they are likely to have at their disposal. Securing a supplementary pension to that provided by the public sector has become essential, given that the latter – across many industrial countries – is set to reduce in value as a proportion of average income. But developing a robust private alternative is proving fraught with dangers for large groups of workers.

This last point was clearly brought out in developments following the Social Security Act of 1986 which, among other things, introduced changes designed to promote DC occupational schemes and personal pensions. This coincided with the rapid growth of financial markets (under the Thatcher administration), with pension provision targeted as a lucrative area for development. The number of people with a personal pension increased significantly from 3.4 million in 1988 to 5.6 million in 1994/5 (Department of Social Security, 1997). Unfortunately, this expansion brought major problems, with the mis-selling of pensions on a huge scale. In the measured tones of *The Times* (16 July 1997):

> The life insurance companies saw the handing over of pensions provisions in the private sector as a golden opportunity to deprive the public of £4 billion. Life insurance salesmen, earning hundreds of thousands in commission, encouraged miners, nurses and other public sector workers to leave schemes with guaranteed benefits to take out plans where the charges in some cases meant that none of the policyholders' contributions were invested for up to four years.

It is estimated that between 1988 and 1993, around 1.5 million pension policies were wrongly sold, with the worst affected duped into leaving attractive index-linked pensions for private plans. Years later, thousands were still unaware of the mistake they had made and that they could be missing out on thousands of pounds for their old age. A report by the UK Office of Fair Trading (OFT) (1997) concluded that many personal pensions were of poor value, with benefits eroded by the high costs of marketing and fund management. The OFT found that up to 30 per cent of a fund could be eaten up by charges over 25 years, with salesmen making inflated claims for the returns from active management of personal pensions to distract attention from high charges. Little has changed since the report from the OFT. Overcharging by the pensions industry has persisted, as has the lack of transparency about the calculation of costs for managing pension funds (Pitt-Watson and Mann, 2012).

Little wonder that a survey conducted in 2006 found that among those with a current personal pension or who had had one in the past, 60 per cent took the view that they were 'too much of a risk' (Clery et al., 2007). The same survey found nearly one in two (47 per cent) respondents (not yet retired) reporting that they 'had no idea' what their retirement income would be (just 10 per cent had a 'good idea'). The National Association of Pension Funds (NAPF) *Workplace Pensions Survey* (2011) reported that 48 per cent of working adults said that they lacked confidence in pensions in comparison to other ways of saving. These findings are reflected in the reduction in the proportion of people of working age contributing to a non-state pension (i.e., an occupational or personal pension). Overall, only 36 per cent of individuals contributed to a private pension in 2008/10. In the case of men, the decline has been from 52 per cent in 1999/2000 down to 37 per cent in 2010/11 (Office for National Statistics [ONS], 2012d). The change is less marked among high-income groups, but is especially apparent among those on low incomes: among people earning between £200 and £300 per week the reduction is from 58 to 34 per cent. These changes reflect both the 'disillusionment' with pensions reported in workplace surveys (Association of Consulting Actuaries, 2012) and the pressures to divert expenditure into paying off debts or meeting other spending priorities. A survey in 2008 found one in ten pension savers planning to take a break in payments during the year, with those aged 25–34 most likely to do so (Brewin Dolphin, 2008). This shift in approach to pensions is reflected at a company level, with one survey reporting that among larger employers (those with 250 or more employees) one-third were looking to reduce their overall spend on pensions (Association of Consulting Actuaries, 2012).

The volatility of non-state provision is illustrated by the decline in occupational pension provision, only partially offset by the growth of personal (DC) pensions. Active membership of occupational pension schemes (both public and private) has reduced from 10.1 million in 2000 to 8.3 million in 2010 – the lowest level since the 1950s (ONS, 2011d). There has been a substantial (and – in terms of rapidity – largely unforeseen) decline in membership of DB schemes. In 2000, active members – i.e., current employees accruing new benefits – in non-government (private sector) DB schemes totalled 4.1 million; this had dropped to 1.0 million by 2010 (ONS, 2011d). This figure was actually below the modelling assumptions used in the UK Pensions Commission (2004) *First Report*, which suggested a long-term floor of around 1.6–1.8 million members. Of final-salary DB schemes in the private sector, 79 per cent are now closed to new employees, compared with just 17 per cent in 2001.

Total pension income (defined as private – including occupational – pensions plus state benefit income) continues to provide 'only modest levels of income for many pensioner households' (ONS, 2008b). Government sources of income remain crucial to sustaining the lives of older people: in 2010–11 state benefits accounted for 43 per cent of their income; occupational pensions comprised 26 per cent, earnings 20 per cent, investment income 7 per cent and personal pensions 4 per cent (Department for Work and Pensions [DWP], 2012). The instability of investment income as a proportion of incomes is especially noteworthy – declining from a peak (as a percentage of average gross incomes of retired households) of 21 per cent in 1991, down to the 2010 figure of 8 per cent. This partly reflected the importance of other elements in pensioner incomes, but also the impact of the economic recession (low interest rates especially) in reducing the value of investments.

Inequality and poverty are other significant dimensions to understanding social ageing. Property ownership and different sources of income continue to serve as the basis for class divisions in late life, similar to those at earlier stages in the life course but reinforced by the class-based nature of occupational benefits. Access to a private (non-state) pension is highly skewed towards the higher socioeconomic groups: 75 per cent of managerial and professionals are members of schemes, compared with 33 per cent of those in routine and semi-routine occupations (ONS, 2012d). The distribution of incomes to pensioners in the UK has widened since 1979, with the increasing value of non-state sources of income leading to a faster growth in incomes towards the top end of the scale. As an illustration, median net income per week for pensioner couples (after housing costs [AHC]) in the bottom fifth of the income distribution was £185 over the three-year period 2008–11, compared with £799 for the top fifth; equivalent figures for single pensioners were £100 and £367 (DWP, 2012). The contrast between groups narrowed somewhat over the 2000s, with a more even distribution of occupational pensions; nonetheless, in 2008–9, 56 per cent of income from such pensions, together with annuities, was taken up by the top income quintile.

Notwithstanding the above, a more positive trend can also be inferred from changes in the financial circumstances of older people. For example, on the standard measure of relative poverty, defined as earnings below 60 per cent of contemporary household income, the period since the mid-1990s has seen fairly consistent falls in pensioner poverty in the UK and other such countries. Using a poverty line of 60 per cent median income, 1.8 million people aged 60/65 and over are living in poverty (AHC) and 2.1 million before housing costs (BHC) (2009–10 figures). Jin et al. (2011: 55) comment on these figures: 'Pensioner poverty is at its lowest level since the first half of the 1980s. In particular, the rate of pensioner poverty has been lower than that in 2009–10 in only two years since the start of our consistent time series in 1961 (1983 and 1984) using incomes measured AHC and in only three years (1982 to 1984) using incomes measured BHC.'

Nonetheless – and while pausing to note that the above figures still mean some two million people (aged 60/65 and over) are unable to participate in society on any reasonable basis – contrasts *within* the older population are important.

The poverty rate for single women aged 70–79 is 26.9 per cent (BHC) compared with 13.7 per cent for men (and 18.5 per cent for pensioners overall). For the oldest-old (80-plus), almost certainly experiencing vulnerability to health and climatic changes, the poverty rate for single women is 25.5 per cent and for men 19.2 per cent (BHC). More than two-thirds of pensioners living in relative poverty are women: in part because there are more female than male pensioners in the older population, and in part because of the low income levels of many women pensioners. Cumulative deprivation plays a significant role, with the low income levels of many women pensioners reflecting both the gender gap in respect of wages and salaries and interrupted work histories due to caring responsibilities.

Ethnicity is a further important dimension in respect of inequalities within the older population. Again using the 60 per cent threshold, while, in the UK, the poverty rate for white pensioners is 20 per cent (BHC) and 16 per cent (AHC), that for Pakistanis and Bangladeshis is 48 per cent and 46 per cent respectively, for Indians 33 and 29 per cent, and for Black Caribbean 28 and 27 per cent. These figures reflect the cumulative disadvantages associated with low-paid work, high levels of unemployment and limited access to occupational and personal pensions as well as the state pension (DWP, 2012).

What emerges from the above summary is that, at least on an income basis, ageing is being constructed in more complex ways than was the case in the 1950s and 1960s. The daily reality for many groups within the older population remains that of living on a very narrow range of income that almost certainly limits participation within the community: among pensioner couples, 28 per cent have no savings, or less than £1,500; among single female pensioners the figure rises to 45 per cent (DWP, 2011b). For single retired individuals, expenditure on housing, fuel and power, and household goods and services comprises around one-quarter of household expenditure, compared with one-sixth for two adult non-retired households with children (2008 figures). Fuel poverty looms as an important issue in the context of climate change and escalating energy costs. Over 30 per cent of the households of single people aged 60-plus in England (1.0

million) are defined as 'fuel poor' (Department of Energy and Climate Change, 2012) with, for the very poorest households, evidence that food expenditure, in periods of very low temperatures, is reduced to pay for extra heating costs (Brimstone, 2011).

Yet in contrast with the above, it is also the case that older households – especially those defined as part of the baby boom generation – are transforming the way in which ageing is experienced in more positive ways. There has been a substantial rise in the proportion of pensioners in the top half of the income distribution – from 25 per cent in 1979 to 50 per cent in 2010/11 (DWP, 2012). Gilleard and Higgs (2011: 365) refer to the way in which older people have become engaged in what they term 'complex' consumption, with many retired households able to access a wide variety of domestic goods and build leisure-based lifestyles around these. Indeed, evidence for this is compelling, with examples such as the rise of the 'second-home industry', tourism and the extensive involvement of older people in cultural and educational activities (the latter illustrated by the growth of the University of the Third Age and associated activities).

But the positive developments identified above run alongside negative features that threaten to undermine beliefs that income security for older people is possible. These are partly linked to the recession following the banking collapse of 2008, but are also associated with the changes to the organization of pensions referred to earlier in this chapter. It is to a review of these that the discussion now turns.

Pension privatization and beliefs about ageing

The trends identified above clearly reflect continuing problems in the provision of pensions for key groups among the working and retired populations. Blackburn (2006: 118) concludes from this analysis:

> Pension provision is a field where commercial provision has been tested and found wanting. After nearly fifty years during which more than half the working population has paid into such schemes – and during which they enjoyed ... vast

subsidies – the modest (US) or miserly (UK) public old-age pension is still the most important source of income for 60 per cent of those in retirement in those countries.

Additionally, developments since the early 2000s suggest a more fundamental shift in approach towards financial support for retirement. This is spelt out by Peston (2008: 255) as follows:

What has happened to corporate pensions funds reflects a change in the culture of the UK, the abandonment of the notion that companies have a moral obligation to promote the welfare of their employees after a lifetime of service. It is part and parcel of the death of paternalism and the rise of individualism. Company directors are no longer asking what it cost them to provide a comfortable retirement for staff. Instead, the majority of big companies are investigating the price of ridding themselves of any responsibility for their retired workforce. This is a less conspicuous but hugely important example of how the wealth of the many is being eroded, while that of the super-rich has soared.

Similarly, in the US, Munnell observes: 'We [are] seeing a brand-new phenomenon: healthy companies are closing their pension plans to existing employees and new employees . . . Employers want out of the benefits game. They just do not want the responsibility of providing pensions' (cited in Greenhouse, 2008: 279). Indeed, in the case of the US, over the period between 1979 and 2009 the share of employees in DB plans fell from 62 per cent to 7 per cent of the total, whereas those in DC plans rose from 16 per cent to 67 per cent.

Stock market-based/DC plans (occupational and personal) have thus become highly important in terms of transforming the landscape of pensions. But their significance lies as much in how they are influencing attitudes to ageing as in their efficiency or otherwise as a vehicle for providing resources for retirement. The rapid expansion of DC pensions has come despite severe inadequacies in the regulatory framework assessing risks for pension scheme members (National Audit Office, 2012). DC schemes have introduced additional areas of complexity to what is already a highly opaque system of financial support. When joining a DC scheme, most individuals (typically 80–90 per cent of scheme members) leave decision-making during the 'accumulation phase' to experts – what is known as a 'default investment strategy'. In other words, workers are disengaged from the business of how their pension is managed over the course of their working lives. This becomes a particular problem when decisions need to be made about how to invest the pot of money produced at the point of retirement. At this stage, there is a transfer of risk onto the shoulders of the individual retiree who, having been 'locked out' of involvement with their scheme, now has to make difficult decisions about annuities and related sources of investment.

Harrison's (2012) review of the DC industry concluded that this 'sudden transfer of risk and responsibility at the point of retirement' was inappropriate and indicated a failure of governance in the running of schemes. Moreover, the net result was often that individuals purchased the wrong type of annuity, often at the wrong price, resulting in reduced income in retirement. Harrison estimated that choosing the wrong sort of annuity resulted in scheme members losing aggregated lifetime income worth between £500 million and £1 billion per annum. She notes (2012: 17):

> Current regulation does not require schemes or providers to ensure members secure the right type of annuity at a fair price. The minimum requirement is that the member is given basic generic information – for example the annuity and [Open Market Option] leaflet . . . Additional governance is optional on the part of scheme providers, employees, the trustees, and their advisers.

For most people, the average amount available from the pension fund to purchase an annuity is relatively small – £25,874 in 2010 – hence decisions about using the money to support long-term needs in retirement will be crucial. The evidence, however, suggests that many retirees will accept an annuity from their own scheme even though interest rates are likely to be lower than those offered on the open market. Harrison (2012: 21) notes that providers may also save money by 'manipulating' the internal rate to make it lower than that on the open market. This has the result of saving money for the provider in situations where a substantial amount of DC funds reach maturity at the same time. Providers – unless specialist advice is available – may also take insufficient account of someone retiring with a limited life expectancy due to a terminal illness. Providing a 'normal' rather than an 'enhanced' annuity means that a smaller amount is taken from the pension fund, resulting in a larger profit for the provider.[2]

Blackburn (2006: 117) summarizes the problems besetting DC schemes in terms of 'uneven coverage, high charges and weak employer commitment'. Wolff (2007), in the US, highlights research linking the rise of DCs with greater wealth inequality and limited coverage among low-wage, part-time and minority workers. Women have particular problems with DCs, with the longevity risk transferred to individual contributors rather than pooled among different groups. Zaidi (2006: 9) observes here:

> [Although] countries have tended to legislate that gender-neutral mortality tables are utilised, there have been practical problems of implementing these annuity regulations with insurance companies reluctant to offer them and the market proving difficult to kick-start. Thus, the net outcome of these reforms increases the risk that women will continue to have lower pension incomes. (See also Blackburn, 2006)

Timmins (2008) highlights the views of one UK investment provider that hundreds of thousands of employees who have been switched out of final-salary pension schemes and into money-purchase products could be on their way to being 'private pension paupers' in old age – with these schemes only replacing around 38 per cent of current salary. This reflects the extent to which employers often contribute fewer resources to their DC plans than is characteristic of traditional DB schemes. Indeed, the switch to DC schemes is invariably accompanied by a review of contribution levels, usually to the detriment of employees.

DC schemes are a particular problem given findings on people's limited understanding of pensions generally; research in the UK shows that two-thirds of respondents claim that their knowledge is 'very patchy' or that they 'know little or nothing' about pensions (cited in DWP, 2008). In the US, Munnell observes: 'Workers have to decide whether to join the [DC] plan, how much to contribute, how much to allocate to what plan, when to change contribution formulas, how to handle things when they move from one job to another. The data show very clearly that many people make mistakes every step of the way' (cited in Greenhouse, 2008: 286). Zaidi (2006: 10), summarizing evidence from Hungary and Poland on the switch from DB to DC schemes, cites surveys which showed how most people felt they were well informed and that information on pension reform was readily available, but that surveys also showed that 'knowledge of the pension system was limited to slogans rather than a deep understanding'. Research conducted by the World Bank also concluded that 'a significant proportion of people simply joined the pension of the first agent they came across' (cited in Zaidi, 2006: 10).

Conclusion: The future of pensions

This chapter has illustrated a number of instabilities affecting pensions in the UK, but with many of the examples relevant to the US as well as countries across Europe. Unsurprisingly, a lively debate is under way about the provision of financial support for old age. In the UK context, substantial legislation has been passed designed to transform the resources provided for retirement. First, the basic state pension (BSP) will be increased each year by average earnings growth, inflation (using the Consumer Price Index) or 2.5 per cent, whichever is higher. Second, automatic enrolment of staff in workplace pensions, designed to assist saving in retirement, is being rolled out from 2012 through to 2018. Alongside this comes a new DC occupational scheme – the National Employment Savings Trust (NEST) – available for employers without a scheme of their own. Third, the state pension age in the UK (in common with many countries) is being progressively raised, with a link now established between pension age and changes in life expectancy. Fourth, a single tier state pension is proposed, to be introduced for all those reaching SPA after 2016.

Viewed from the perspective being developed in this book, such reforms raise a number of concerns. First, they take as axiomatic the desirability of working additional years: this is viewed as acceptable given increased life expectancy and necessary as a means of reducing the cost of pensions. But this measure is especially unfair on working-class groups whose lower life expectancy means they will draw their pension for a significantly shorter period than their managerial and professional counterparts. Blackburn (2006: 53) summarizes the issues as follows:

> The unfairness of class differentials is compounded by the fact that most manual workers, having missed out on further education, started work three or four years earlier than the more long-lived graduate employees, so that those with the longest contribution records receive fewer benefits. Any increase in retirement ages will simply increase these injustices.

Second, pension reforms continue to rest on assumptions about the stability and equity of defined contribution schemes to supplement public pensions. But the actual record – since the 1990s – does little to inspire confidence that those who most need additional income – women, those on low incomes, minority groups – will benefit from such provision. Ginn (2012) identifies a number of concerns for women relating to NEST, including the exclusion of many low-paid part-time workers, the level of contribution required, which may be unaffordable in periods of low pay and the difficulty of making an assessment as to whether staying in a scheme is worthwhile given the potential loss of means-tested benefits. On the last point, one UK analyst describes the NEST scheme as a 'scandal in the making', with lower-paid workers receiving 'negative returns' on their contributions once means-tested benefits are taken into account (*Financial Times*, 9 June 2008). Faced with relatively high contributions and uncertain returns, the likelihood is that large numbers of workers will simply opt out of NEST or similar schemes – smaller firms are budgeting for a rate of up to 30–40 per cent (Association of Consulting Actuaries, 2012).

Third, despite limited recognition of time spent in unpaid care, it will almost certainly remain the case that many groups of women will continue to fare less well in comparison with men even with the reforms to pensions. Low pay and limited private pensions for part-time workers will continue to reflect the predominance of what Meyer and Herd (2007) refer to as 'market friendly' rather than 'family friendly' social and economic polices (see also Estes, 2006).

What are some of the responses that might be made to the issues identified in this chapter? First, it is essential to rebuild confidence that governments can provide protection and support in old age – fundamental elements to any system of social insurance. In the UK, just 14 per cent of respondents in a national survey were 'confident' that the government would provide them with sufficient income in retirement (Clery et al., 2007). This reflects the deep-rooted crisis in the pensions system as described in this chapter, with many working-age people (and older people themselves) caught between doubts about government provision, on the one side, and market-generated support, on the other. Restoring belief that adequate protection for old age is achievable is a fundamental task for any society, but one which many prosperous industrial societies are failing to achieve at the present time.

Second, public provision such as the BSP in the UK remains a fundamental building block in financing a secure old age. However, it is essential that the pension provided not only eliminates poverty but also provides an adequate replacement rate in relation to previous wages and salaries. This raises a fundamental challenge given the direction of policy at the present time. The proposed single-tier state pension (STP) will bring together the BSP and the additional state pension for those reaching SPA after 2016. This will almost certainly raise incomes for many groups of women, lifting them above income-related benefits such as guaranteed credit (GC). However, given the level at which the STP is likely to be set, many will still be eligible for various means-tested benefits. Moreover, with around one-third of women likely to be short of the 30 years of contribution required to receive a full STP, poverty in old age will continue to be a feature of growing old well into the twenty-first century. This underlines the importance of securing public pension provision which compensates for periods of caring and low wages, and which lifts people clear of the need to claim for means-tested benefits. This is likely to become more, not less, desirable if the weakness of DC schemes continue to be exposed and 'opting out' from NEST reaches the level predicted by many employers and experts in the field.

Third, a new global discourse on pensions is required, one which challenges the view that government provision should be reduced and reliance upon the market increased. The experience thus far indicates that market provision has led to a deepening of inequalities among different groups of workers and pensioners, that significant groups are likely to remain without the support of a viable additional pension, and that the volatility of the market is in direct contradiction to the need for security and certainty in old age. This discourse will need to challenge the neo-liberal consensus around pensions, adopted in IGOs such as the World Bank, the International Monetary Fund and the OECD (Estes and Phillipson, 2003). These bodies have been able to exert considerable influence on the pension debate, but one which has marginalized views regarding the necessity of substantial public sector provision.

Finally, generating a new debate on pensions will require the construction (or reconstruction) of a politics of ageing which draws upon the energies of older people themselves, a group largely excluded from discussions around the design of pensions. Yet one of the most serious consequences of the privatization of pensions has been the undermining of confidence in the possibility of achieving security in old age. Doubts about the point of planning or saving for retirement are now widespread – certainly in the UK but in many other countries as well. This is itself reinforced by the lack of transparency in the management of pension schemes, with the alienation of consumers leading to a progressive loss of faith in the system as a whole (Pitt-Watson and Mann, 2012).

All of the above hugely corrodes the possibility of rebuilding a new type of ageing. The outcome will almost certainly be a 'free enterprise old age' with large groups excluded from any kind of dignity and security, albeit with a minority able to continue without much change to their lifestyles in their middle years and into retirement. The material context of ageing does, however, need to be related to the social relationships around which the lives of older people are built. Of these, family and intergenerational ties continue to form a major component, and it is to a discussion of these that we now turn.

7

Families and Generational Change in Ageing Societies

Introduction

The previous chapter examined the way in which retirement and the welfare state had been influential in the construction of ageing through the twentieth century. This chapter examines another important relationship around which the lives of older people have been built – namely that relating to families and generations. Some of the key questions explored in research in recent years have concerned issues relating to the emergence of new forms of multigenerational support, the characteristics of intergenerational solidarity, and changing roles and relationships within families (Bengtson, 1993; Fokkema et al., 2008). This literature has raised important issues about changes affecting the lives of older people both within and without the sphere of family relationships. Equally, the relationships and concerns affecting older people within the family are an important part of the construction of ageing – indeed, viewed from an historical perspective, these have probably formed the most important element in terms of experiences of growing old.

Given the above, the purpose of this chapter is to consider – from a sociological perspective – the range of social ties that underpin population ageing in the twenty-first century. To be sure, the social context of ageing changed dramatically over the course of the twentieth century, with some of the key changes highlighted in the previous chapters. From one standpoint, such changes could be considered as more negative than positive. Older people, it is suggested, are now more 'isolated' from their families than once was the case. Changes associated with rapid globalization are said to be weakening rather than strengthening family ties. Generations are viewed as increasingly in conflict rather than working with each other, illustrated by tensions over the distribution of economic and social resources. All these points are familiar in discussions about the social consequences of ageing societies. From a sociological perspective, however, such assertions must be treated with caution: are families really changing to the degree that is claimed? What evidence is there for the claim that generations are working against each others' interests? To what extent are new types of relationships forming through globalization? How is family life in old age changing under the social and economic pressures associated with the 'risk society'? These and related questions form the main themes reviewed in this chapter. The first section considers the various meanings associated with the term 'generation'. The second section reviews some of the influences of demographic changes on social relationships in later life. We then consider various aspects of globalization and family change. Finally, the chapter will return to assess the nature of intergenerational ties and the possibility of these contributing to conflict or cohesion in the twenty-first century.

Generations and population ageing

The relationship between generations and ageing raises complex issues for social analysis. Bengtson and Putney (2006: 20) make the point: 'The problem of generations and ageing, and the resulting problems of generational succession, support, stability and change, represents one of the most enduring puzzles about social organization and behaviour.' Three main issues can be identified: first, the problem of families or societies ensuring continuity given changes in membership through birth, ageing and generational succession; second, the question of how generations can adapt to a changing social and environmental context; third, the issue of dealing with conflicts or tensions between generations.

The idea of generations has often in fact been taken as an entry point for discussion about influences on social behaviour, whether as a means of understanding political upheaval (e.g. Mannheim, 1952), cultural change (Gilleard and Higgs, 2005) or conflict between age groups (Foner, 2000). Yet these debates have to some extent obscured rather than clarified the links between ageing and generations. In the first place, the conceptual language surrounding generations is often used in different and contradictory ways. Hagestad and Uhlenberg (2007) highlight the fact that three types of phenomena have been assigned the term *generation*: first, *age groups* or individuals at given life stages, such as youth, adulthood and old age; second, *historical generations*, defined as birth cohorts with particular characteristics; third, *family generations* – that is, locations in a system of ranked descent. This discussion follows Hagestad and Uhlenberg (2007: 239–40) in using the last of these to define generations. The authors point out: 'In focusing on these three, one is examining people who not only are anchored differently in dimensions of time, primarily biographical time/chronological age and historical time, but also the rhythm of family time . . . A host of challenging, yet neglected issues lies in the intersection of these three phenomena.'

The discussion in this chapter will also integrate concepts reviewed in the discussion on social theories of ageing in Chapter 3, in particular those relating to *life course analysis* and *globalization*. These concepts will be used to examine what Hagestad and Uhlenberg (2007: 240) refer to as a neglected question in the study of the changing age composition of populations, namely, 'the consequences of population ageing for social relationships'. The discussion will give particular emphasis to questions relating to intergenerational patterns of reciprocity and exchange, locating these within the broader context of globalization and associated changes affecting the life course. In the next section, we will consider the influence of demography on generational and family relationships, highlighting important changes over the course of the twentieth and early part of the twenty-first century.

Demographic and generational change

Chapter 2 provided a summary of the main characteristics of what was termed the 'first demographic revolution', where the impact of declining mortality followed by declining fertility was explored, these elements transforming the shape of populations and the generational groups within them. Fewer deaths and fewer births have resulted in intergenerational structures that are less pronounced at the bottom and much more so at the top. *Horizontal ties* (to siblings, cousins) are reduced in number; *vertical ties* expanded (e.g. from grandparent to grandchild) in scope and complexity. This pattern has been strengthened through continuing falls in mortality affecting most countries of the global north and increasingly those in the global south.

Such developments have increased the availability of extended intergenerational kin (Bengtson and Putney, 2006), with grandparents, to take one example, now more prominent within family relationships (Arber and Timonen, 2012). Hagestad and Uhlenberg (2007: 244) highlight this point with data from the US, giving the number of living grandparents for 10- and 30-year-olds: the proportion of 10-year-olds with all four grandparents alive increased from 6 per cent in 1900 to 41 per cent in 2000; at age 30 just 1 per cent had between two and three grandparents alive in 1900, this increasing to 31 per cent in 2000 (see Grundy et al., 1999 for similar UK data). The co-longevity of different generations is now an important dimension of family life. A study of the first-wave UK baby boom generation (i.e., those born between 1945 and 1952), using data from the English Longitudinal Study of Ageing (ELSA; see Banks et al., 2010), found 43 per cent of those aged 50–57 still had a mother alive (average age 79.8 years) and 20 per cent had a father alive (average age 80.7 years) (Leach et al., 2008). Multi-generational ties now occupy a considerable part of people's lives, with, for example, 40–50 per cent of those aged 80-plus in Continental and North European countries living in four generational groups.

Evidence for what Bengtson et al. (2003) refer to as 'longer years of shared lives' appear matched by the extent of contact and support across generations. Research suggests that the majority of older people remain part of a substantial kin network comprising spouses/partners, children, grandchildren and siblings (Phillipson et al., 2000). Close relationships may be more geographically dispersed but the extent of change can be exaggerated. A survey conducted in Britain in 1999 found around half those aged 50-plus had non-resident children living within 30 minutes' travel time (Grundy et al., 1999). Levels of interaction between older people and their children and other relatives remain extensive. A UK survey published in 2004 reported three-quarters of older people (77 per cent) saw relatives at least weekly, with around one in ten seeing relatives less than once a year (Victor et al., 2004). Fokkema et al. (2008), drawing upon data from the Survey of Health and Retirement in Europe (SHARE) carried out in 11 European countries, reported that 'no more than one per cent of parents had completely lost touch with their children'. Summarizing the state of European families and links between parents and adult children, the same study concluded that 'the majority of European later-life families are characterised by (1) having a child nearby; (2) being in frequent contact with at least one of their children; (3) having strong family care obligations, and (4) regular exchange of help in kind from parents to children'.

Given the above findings, the first demographic transition might be said to have transformed the structure of populations (creating more living generations) but maintained existing patterns of reciprocity and support. Indeed, one argument might be that with older adults (i.e., grandparents) in greater supply but with fewer grandchildren (given declining fertility), the possibilities for support across generations has never been greater. At the same time, it is important not to isolate demographic change from the social and economic structures with which it intersects. In this respect, it might be argued that in the 'first transition', exchange across generations was supported both through the *demographic capital* of increased vertical ties and through the *social capital* produced through the organization of the life course and the development of the welfare state. The welfare state in fact played a vital role in moderating the relationship between generations. Indeed, research from the mid-1990s onwards confirmed that public transfers appeared not to '*crowd out*' support from within the family; rather, there was an element of '*crowding in*', with older generations 'retaining a crucial role in distributing financial and material resources within the family' (Hoff and Tesch-Römer, 2007: 77).

The issue now to be considered is the extent to which the structure and assumptions underpinning intergenerational reciprocity are presently being challenged. To what extent is a period of rapid globalization transforming traditional relationships across generations? What other factors can be cited which might be interacting with the political and social forces generated by global change? To what degree are generations being redefined in the context of familial, social and global transformations? The next section summarizes some of the key changes affecting family life through the life course, linking these to changes in social networks and the importance of personal communities in the lives of older people.

Changing family ties and social ageing

The question of family ties has long been a major concern in the study of ageing. Research on this topic in Britain by Townsend (1957) in the 1950s and Shanas (1979) in the US in the 1960s and 1970s, was influential in setting an agenda that explored patterns of care and support in a context of greater geographical and social mobility (Litwak, 1960). This work examined the social world of older people as dominated by families first of all, friends and neighbours second and voluntary and bureaucratic organizations a distant third (to paraphrase the formulation expressed in the 1970s by Shanas).

By the turn of the twenty-first century, however, the extent of family change, illustrated by 'reconstituted families', the impact of divorce and the trend towards living alone, was raising major new questions for the sociology of family life applied to ageing. The range of experiences now contained within the institution of the family appeared to be 'loosening' ties between generations. Bernades (cited in Allan and Crow, 2001) asked the question, 'Do we really know what "the family" is?', the answer to which appeared rather less clear than it was when Parsons (1943) was developing his model of the 'nuclear family' in the 1930s and 1940s. In some ways, the idea that family practices had become less predictable and more diverse created uncertainty among those involved in studying ageing populations. Shanas's (1979) argument that the family was invariably the first line of support had become embedded within the core assumptions made by students of ageing, mirrored in part by neo-liberal social policies focusing on family support as a major line of defence in the provision of care for older people.

The issue of diversity had also been sidelined by the main theoretical tradition used to explain family relationships. Social exchange theory, along with the related concept of reciprocity, has been employed in numerous studies of the family life of older people. Lowenstein (1999: 400) summarizes this approach as follows:

> In the study of intergenerational relations, there is an increased emphasis on the interdependence of generations, that is the mutual exchange of resources between elderly parents and their adult children, based on social exchange theory. Social exchange theory deals with the balance between dependence and power as an important determinant of the satisfaction which two persons experience in their relationship.

As broad principles underpinning social relationships, ideas about exchange and reciprocity continue to exert considerable force. They have been especially important in the debate about intergenerational equity, and have been used to explain a number of findings from research in the area of family sociology (e.g. Arber and Attias-Donfut, 2000; Lowenstein and Katz, 2010). At the same time, this approach may need some modification given a context of greater fluidity and instability in personal relationships (Settersten and Trauten, 2009). Reciprocity in the 'risk society', as advanced by Beck (1992), may have a different quality when compared with the 'environment of kin' (Frankenberg, 1966) into which older people's lives have traditionally been placed. Gouldner's (1960) argument about the universality of reciprocity may still apply, but the associated mechanisms – given globalization – are likely to produce different outcomes for kin as well as non-kin relations (see further below).

The possibility of open or porous kinship boundaries has been a significant theme in the research literature. Stack's (1974) study of an African American urban community in the US demonstrated how standard definitions of nuclear or extended families often failed to capture the complexity of daily life. Added to this is the importance of demographic changes such as later age of marriage, delayed childbirth and cohabitation, all of which underline the significance of the view that there can be 'little doubt that the network of potentially significant relationships is becoming enlarged' (Riley and Riley, 1993: 187; Chambers et al., 2009).

The rise of 'personal communities'

A key issue for discussion concerns identifying the appropriate level of analysis for understanding changes in relationships. Generational perspectives are vital when tracing developments at the macro-economic and macro-social levels, as the debate around intergenerational equity and the link between family and welfare generations demonstrates (Hills, 1996). But this must be complemented by approaches better able to explore micro-social developments, especially in respect of the process and dynamics of family and community change. Here, the concept of 'personal communities' (i.e., the world of friends, neighbours, leisure-associates and kin) has some merit when attempting to capture the interplay of different kinds of social ties in old age. Wellman and Wortley (1990: 560) define a 'personal community network' as:

> a person's set of active community ties, [which] is usually socially diverse, spatially dispersed, and sparsely knit . . . its ties vary in characteristics and in the kinds of support they provide. Until now, community (and kinship) analysts have concentrated on documenting the persistence, composition, and structure of these networks in order to show that

community has not been lost in contemporary societies. They have paid less attention to evaluating how characteristics of community ties and networks affect access to the supportive resources that flow through them.

The development of 'personal communities' illustrates what may be termed the 'voluntaristic' element in personal relations. Instead of people being locked into family groups, they may be more accurately perceived as 'managing' a spread (or 'convoy', to use Kahn and Antonucci's [1980] term) of relationships, with friends, kin, neighbours and other supporters exchanging and receiving help at different points of the life course (Pahl, 2000; Lowenstein and Katz, 2010; Phillipson et al., 2000). Viewing people as 'managers' of a network of relationships offers a different approach from that usually adopted in studies of social ageing. Here, the focus has been upon a preordained sequence starting with the family and leading out towards other sets of relationships. However, an alternative approach is to view older people as 'active' network participants, adopting a range of 'strategies' and 'practices' in maintaining social ties (Chambers et al., 2009).

The move towards 'voluntaristic' ties reflects important developments in the experience of ageing in the twenty-first century. Demographic changes will almost certainly lead, as Bengtson et al. (2003) suggest, to the increased salience of multigenerational ties, with bonds of friendship complementing these but also in some cases substituting for kin-based support. Moreover, this may be especially characteristic of the baby boom generation, in particular those born in the late 1940s and early 1950s and now entering retirement. In the UK, the marriage and divorce patterns of the first-wave baby boom generation marks a distinct change from preceding cohorts. They provide early indicators of the growth of divorce and re-partnering characteristic of the post-war family, with data from the English Longitudinal Study of Ageing showing 35 per cent of those born between 1945 and 1952 in a category other than 'first and only marriage' or 'widowed'; equivalent figures for those born in 1937–44 and 1929–36 were 31 per cent and 23 per cent, respectively. First-wave baby boomers also indicate a distinct break over these preceding cohorts in the proportion who have lived at some point with a partner without being married, with nearly one in five among those born between 1945 and 1954 compared with an average of fewer than one in ten in the preceding cohorts (Leach et al., 2008).

The impact of these changes was highlighted in SHARE data analysed by Fokkema et al. (2008); they noted that social class as well as demographic variables influenced contact and support within the family. In addition, they found, for example, that parental divorce and higher social class contributed to a weakening of parent–child ties:

> [D]ivorced single parents and the more highly educated and wealthier parents are living at a greater distance from their children and having less frequent contact and weaker feelings of family care obligations than their counterparts. Moreover, divorced mothers and fathers and parents with higher incomes are less likely to receive help in kind from their children than widows/widowers and those with low incomes, respectively. (Fokkema et al., 2008: iv)

Hughes and Waite (2007: 196) suggest that more recent cohorts such as the baby boomers look very different from earlier ones:

> Members of later cohorts are less likely to be currently married, more likely to be living alone, and more likely to be living in a complex household. The incidence of cohabitation, multiple marriages, and non-marital childbearing and child-lessness will all be greater in these cohorts than in earlier ones . . . Along with these differences in family structures have come both new and altered family roles and relationships. Most importantly, these changes appear to have challenged people's ideas of what constitutes a family and what family members may or may not owe each other. (See also Chambers et al., 2009; Treas and Marcum, 2011)

Such expectations are, however, also being transformed by the changes associated with globalization and the rise of what have been termed 'transnational communities'. As we move through the twenty-first century, the 'globalization of people' will become an increasingly important dimension to trans-forming many aspects of ageing societies. The next section summarizes some of the main changes associated with global economic and social change.

The rise of transnational communities

Schiller et al. (1992: 5) defined transnationalism as:

> [the process by which] immigrants build social fields that link together their country of origin and their country of settlement. Immigrants who build such social fields are designated 'transnational migrants'. Transnational migrants develop and maintain multiple relations – familial, economic, social, organizational, religious, and political that span borders. They take actions, make decisions, and feel concerns, and develop identities within social networks that connect them to two or more societies simultaneously.

In similar vein, Basch et al. (1994: 6) define this relationship as follows:

> '[T]transnationalism' [is] the process by which immigrants forge and sustain multi-stranded social relations that link together their societies of origin and settlement. We call these processes transnationalism to emphasize that many immigrants build social fields that cross geographic, cultural and political borders . . . an essential element is the multiplicity of involvements that transmigrants sustain in home and host societies.

Transnational communities may themselves be said to reflect both the growth of a global economy and the impact of this on the construction of family and community ties. This new political economy is creating what may be described as 'global families', which arise from the communities that emerge from international migration. A significant group comprise those who came as labour migrants (or as the wives thereof) to countries such as Britain and who have subsequently 'aged in place' (Warnes et al., 2004). Many of these, however, even among the very poor, and especially among the first generation of migrants, may return at regular intervals to their country of origin (Gardner, 1995). As a consequence, globalization is producing a new kind of generational structure in which the dynamics of family and social life may be stretched across different continents and societies.

Global migration is also producing considerable diversity in respect of the social networks within which growing old is shaped and managed. Typically, older people's networks have been examined within national borders, with experiences of care and support assessed in this context (Phillipson, 1998). But migrants bring important variations with responsibilities that may cover considerable physical as well as cultural distances. King and Vullnetari (2006), for example, explored the impact of the mass migration of young people from Albania, notably on those older people living in rural parts of the country. They report feelings of separation and abandonment among the older generation, heightened by the realization that their children are unlikely to return (Vullnetari and King, 2008). The Albanian case illustrates problems of maintaining ties with relatives who may have entered a destination country without having any legal position, with their 'undocumented status making it difficult for them to return' to their homeland country (Vullnetari and King, 2008: 788).

In contrast to the above, there are numerous examples in the literature of migrants moving 'backwards and forwards' between their 'first' and 'second' homeland, subject to financial and domestic constraints. Goulbourne (1999) highlighted the 'back and forth' movement of Caribbean families living in Britain (see also Bauer and Thompson, 2006). Similar descriptions have been linked to first-generation Bangladeshi migrants in the UK (Gardner, 2002; Phillipson et al., 2003); to Italian migrants in Perth, Western Australia (Baldasser et al., 2007); and to members of the Turkish community living in Germany (Buffel and Phillipson, 2012). All this movement reflects what Christine Ho (1991) has described, in her research on Anglo-Trinidadians living in Los Angeles, as 'the concerted effort [of migrants] to sustain connections across time and geography'.

This type of movement, across time and space, raises complex issues for the maintenance of what was referred to earlier as 'intergenerational reciprocity'. On the one hand,

Baldassar (2007) challenges traditional assumptions that support is necessarily grounded in physical proximity between the individuals concerned. She goes on to note: 'Empirically, the general preoccupation with geographic proximity means that very little research has been done on the relationships between ageing parents and adult children who live at a distance . . . with the result that transnational practices of care have remained largely invisible or assumed to be unfeasible.' Following this, if we recognize the different dimensions associated with care and support – practical, financial, personal, emotional and moral – then distinctive possibilities emerge for maintaining a caring relationship of one kind or another across national boundaries.

At the same time, it is important to recognize the pressures and constraints affecting families dispersed across the globe as a consequence of migration. Bauer and Thompson (2006: 5), in their study of Jamaican migrants, suggest:

> [There is] a kind of grief intrinsic in migration itself, even when made in a spirit of betterment. Some migrants for years continued to feel a general sense of loss, which they expressed in terms of feeling physically isolated. Migrant women were particularly likely to feel the absence of family and close local community at times of child birth, but sometimes men spoke of similar feelings of loss.

Baldassar (2007) argues, however, that such feelings will vary across different groups, reflecting, for example, whether they come from earlier or later cohorts of migrants and stages of the family life cycle. She studied three cohorts of Italian migrants to Perth (Western Australia): those who left, first, in the 1950s and 1960s; second, in the 1970s and 1980s; and, third, in the 1990s. It was the second group, most of whom had reached their fifties in the 2000s, who were experiencing the greatest difficulties in supporting parents in their first homeland:

> [This group] expressed the greatest concerns for ageing parents and providing care from a distance. Many have parents who can no longer speak on the phone due to dementia or who can no longer write due to disability . . . Even those parents who are in good health consider visiting Perth too hazardous

or are busy caring for an ailing spouse. This state of affairs generally results in this group being engaged in more intense 'distant thinking' and more frequent visits than the post-war cohort, whose parents are now deceased. Women, in particular, struggle with feelings of guilt about their inability to provide more support for their parents and to their siblings who are caring for parents. (Baldassar, 2007: 290)

These experiences will almost certainly increase given the accelerated migration of people from rural to urban areas, occurring in many parts of the world (Arnold, 2012). The consequences of these shifts in population will be an important factor contributing to changes in the nature of support within families and generations (Chambers et al., 2009)

Social ageing and social capital

In sociological terms, the arguments developed above take us back to ideas about community and solidarity developed by Marx, Weber, Durkheim and Simmel. Wellman (1998), for example, notes that while this tradition highlighted the crisis in relationships accompanying the rise of modern capitalism, the potential for new communal ties was acknowledged in classical sociology through concepts such as 'organic solidarity' (Durkheim, 1933) and through research in the field of urban sociology. The idea of relationships being reconstructed in an urbanizing society was, however, neglected by research in ageing, mainly because of the preoccupation with families as the main line of contact and support. However, the issue that now needs to be considered is not just the possibility of alternatives to kin (see further below), but the idea of new forms of cooperation around which the future of ageing might be built. One way of approaching this issue is through the notion of social capital as developed in the writings of Bourdieu (1986), Coleman (1990), Putnam (2000) and others. In his review of this concept, Portes (1998: 7) suggests that '[a] consensus is growing in the literature that social capital stands for the ability of actors to secure benefits by virtue of membership in social networks or other social structures'. He writes:

> Both Bourdieu and Coleman emphasize the intangible char-
> acter of social capital relative to other forms. Where economic
> capital is in people's bank accounts and human capital is
> inside their heads, social capital inheres in the structure of
> their relationships. To possess social capital, a person must be
> related to others, and it is those others, not himself who are
> the actual source of his or her disadvantage.

Ideas about social capital also draw upon Granovetter's (1973) distinction between 'strong' and 'weak' ties, the former referring to the 'dense' ties to family and those similar to oneself, the latter to individuals dissimilar to oneself. A related distinction is between 'bonding' and 'bridging' forms of social capital, the former important for mobilizing social solidarity and support, the latter gaining access to new resources and identities (Putnam, 2000).

Studies of ageing have tended to focus upon the value of 'strong ties' – for example, those linked to immediate family and long-lasting friends and neighbours. Strong ties have the virtue of social inclusion; equally, reliance on these alone may risk people being marginalized or cut off from other groups. Just as people may need a spread of ties for accessing help in securing employment or promotion, scattered and episodic ties may be helpful in assisting people through periods such as retirement and old age. Pahl and Spencer (1997: 37) make the general point that 'those who have emphasised old-style ties based on gender, race or ethnicity as a way of empower-ing disadvantaged categories may unwittingly have added to their troubles by making it more difficult for such close-knit groups to develop "bridging" ties'. Such ties may be espe-cially significant to the widow seeking alternatives to kin for support, to men and women entering retirement seeking to engage with new lifestyles and to those needing help from abusive and exploitative relationships.

At a broader level, the argument also concerns older peo-ple's engagement with a 'de-traditionalized' world, with the reconstruction of later life as a period of choice on the one side, but one of risk and danger on the other. Inclusive ties fit well with inclusive institutions such as the welfare state, a stable intergenerational contract and fixed-age compulsory retirement. Given the fragmentation of these into multiple pathways or privatized forms, a mix of strong and weak ties may become more advantageous. Empirically, the task becomes that of documenting the combination of ties generated in the diverse settings and communities in which people live their lives. Multigenerational ties will almost certainly be part of these, but may be complemented as well by other (non-blood) types of relationships.

Conclusion: Globalization and the future of intergenerational relations

How will the various changes documented in this chapter influence ageing and intergenerational ties over the course of the twenty-first century? Bengtson and Putney (2006: 21), in their review of this area, suggest that relations between age groups have indeed become more problematic, given a context of globalization and rapid social change. Yet they also suggest that intergenerational relations may be the key to resolving many of the associated problems:

> This is because the essential characteristics of multigenerational families – relatedness, interdependence and solidarity, and age integration – can influence and transform societal practices and policies and mitigate potential for conflicts between age groups. In matters of relations between generations and age, there are strong common characteristics between multigenerational families, age groups and society. A viable social contract between generations will remain a characteristic of human society in the future – at both the micro and macro levels of age group interactions.

But the possibilities for tensions and divisions should also be noted. At the micro level, there is increasing fluidity as well as diversity in family life. Morgan (1996), for example, makes the point that rather than simply following established cultural principles or norms governing ways of doing and being a family, individuals are active in creating their own modes of living. These may or may not meet principles of solidarity and interdependence, but will almost certainly reflect the outcome of actions 'negotiated' (to use Finch and Mason's [1993] phrase) between family members. And the degree of age integration can itself be overemphasized, with studies by Uhlenberg and De Jong Gierveld (2004: 22) suggesting 'a deficit of young adults in the networks of older people' (see also Hagestad and Uhlenberg, 2007). At a macro level, relations between generations may come under pressure from a variety of directions. Problems with pension funding, given the long-run decline in the working population and the (at least) short-run economic recession, are already leading to a return to debates about generational equity (see Chapter 7). And globalization has the capacity to arouse more generalized fears which may themselves corrode trust between generations. Tony Judt (2008: 20) expressed this point as follows:

> Fear is reemerging as an active ingredient of political life in Western democracies. Fear of terrorism, of course; but also and perhaps most insidiously, fear of uncontrollable speed of change, fear of the loss of employment, fear of losing ground to others in an increasingly unequal distribution of resources, fear of losing control of the circumstances and routines of one's daily life. And, perhaps above all, fear that it is not just we who can no longer shape our lives but that those in authority have lost control as well to forces beyond their reach.

Given the above context, intergenerational relationships may be entering a period of considerable uncertainty and upheaval. Ageing populations, and the vulnerable groups within them, need the certainty of predictable incomes and services. Yet, these are not yet available to the mass of older people in developing countries, and their supply appears increasingly precarious to those in the developed world. Making the intergenerational contract work to resolve these issues will be increasingly important in the years ahead. Strengthening intergenerational relations given the insecurities arising from global change remains an essential social and public policy objective.

But against the negative points, positive developments might also be noted, reflecting the development of new forms of social capital. First, the rise of 'personal communities', as highlighted in this chapter, suggests that a broader spread of relationships may now be available at all stages of the life course (see Chapter 10). And the baby boom generation – with much more diverse relationships compared with previous cohorts – suggests that patterns of exchange and support are more likely to be built around a mix of kin and non-kin ties.

Second, another important development will be the further application of various forms of technology to complement existing relationships and traditional forms of support. Treas and Marcum (2011: 137) note:

> Distance has always mattered for maintaining relationships, but technology decreases its significance for many forms of interaction . . . Even face-to-face interaction is possible with video-chat services, but the need for in-person contact may diminish as technology changes the content of interactions. For instance, the 1990s increase in older adults' use of assistive technology (grab bars, walkers, etc.) coincided with declines in the personal care (e.g. help with bathing) often provided in person by kin.

Third, mobility and migration will be important in transforming the nature of social ageing. Baby boomers may prefer to 'age in place' (see Chapter 9), even as they continue to spend long periods outside their principal home (in the UK nearly 20 per cent of middle-class and upper-class baby boomers own a second home – many of these outside the UK). Linked with this may be the importance of consumerism for those sections of the baby boom generation able to maintain continuity in lifestyles from work to retirement (Gilleard and Higgs, 2011). A more nomadic form of ageing may become characteristic for many such groups, built around travel and related pursuits. Against this, the reality for many will be rather more modest expectations about ageing, given challenges to their financial position and problems relating to the provision of health and social care. The next chapter turns to a discussion of this area, especially in the context of issues faced by people in 'late' old age.

8
'Late' Old Age

Introduction

The last 100 years have seen major developments in the age composition of older people. The demographic basis was outlined in Chapter 2, with the increase in those aged 80 and over the most notable dimension of the changes discussed. This area – the social implications of people living into what has been termed 'late old age' – remains relatively unexplored territory in the field of sociology as compared with social policy. The argument outlined by Robert Butler (1975: 1), in his pioneering study *Why Survive? Being Old in America*, remains valid for many aspects of sociological research:

> Aging is the neglected stepchild of the human life cycle. Though we have begun to examine the socially taboo subjects of dying and death, we have leaped over that long period of time preceding death known as old age. In truth, it is easier to manage the problem of death than the problem of living as an older person. Death is a dramatic, one-time crisis while old age is a day-to-day and year-by-year confrontation with powerful external and internal forces, a bittersweet coming to terms with one's own personality and one's life.

Of course, the ageing process has hardly been under-researched since the time that Butler was writing. Indeed, the range of work covered by the various disciplines working within gerontology amounts to what is now a huge industry devoted to understanding the impact of ageing populations. Yet one might still argue that the sociological understanding of ageing – especially as applied to late old age – is at an early stage of development (Grenier, 2012). Health and related changes affecting people in their 70s, 80s and beyond have invariably been the subject of extensive discussion. Where there is acknowledgement of social dimensions, the discussion – as Hagestad and Dannefer (2001) suggest – largely occurs at the 'micro level', exploring the psycho-social characteristics of individuals embedded within family and friendship-based networks. Of equal importance, however, are macro-level perspectives on ageing, and the role of social institutions and social structures in shaping the way in which later life is experienced. The task here is to think about ageing beyond the individual level, placing it within the more general context of influences and changes associated with living in a global society.

The argument developed in this chapter is that the changes reviewed at different points of this book are now having a profound influence on the experience of late old age, in particular the extent to which – following Townsend (1981) – this period can be viewed as one of 'structured dependency' or one where new forms of interdependence might be developed. To continue the argument developed at different points of this book, the transformation in the social context within which older people live their lives holds out a mixture of positive and negative features in respect of expectations about quality of life in late old age. To explore this theme, the chapter first examines aspects of the construction of late old age; second, it reviews aspects of the medicalization of ageing; third, it examines issues relating to the health and social care of people in late old age; finally, it summarizes some of the themes discussed in the context of a number of questions and dilemmas for late old age.

Constructing late old age

Previous chapters have illustrated the extent to which what became taken-for-granted from the mid–late twentieth century

– the development of secure pensions and a stable welfare state – became weakened and fragmented in the early part of the twenty-first century. Both elements are now far less predictable and uncertain for the cohort now experiencing late old age and for those approaching this final period of the life course. From the perspective of this book, the final stages of the life course highlights central themes of sociological analysis, in particular those relating to social integration and cohesion as well as issues relating to identity and inequality (Dannefer, 2011). Such questions have assumed greater relevance given the changes discussed in earlier chapters. On the one side, the erosion of distinct phases within the life course and the creation of more fluid transitions from mid-life and beyond have produced uncertainty about the character of later life. The social purpose of retirement and ageing has become 'disembedded' from traditional sources of meaning, whether in the idea of a 'secure retirement' or 'dignified old age'. Both now seem open to questioning given global and economic pressures running through western society. On the other side, the inevitably of particular health conditions towards the end of life (cancer, cardiovascular disease, musculoskeletal problems) and the clustering of deaths after the age of 75 creates a particular type of certainty and predictability.

Understanding experiences towards the end of life has also become a problem, in part because of the emphasis placed upon maintaining 'active' and 'successful' ageing for as long as possible (World Heath Organization, 2001). Both these elements have become associated with what is known as 'the third age', a period separated from the responsibilities of working life and the infirmities linked with 'late old age' or the 'fourth age' (Laslett, 1989). Weiss and Bass (2002: 3) have outlined the characteristics of these periods as follows:

> The life phase in which there is no longer employment and childraising to commandeer time, and before morbidity enters to limit activity and mortality brings everything to a close, has been called the Third Age. Those in this phase of life have passed through a first age of youth, when they prepared for the activities of maturity, and a second age of maturity, when their lives were given to those activities, and have reached a third age in which they can, within fairly wide limits, live their lives as they please, before being taken over by a fourth age of decline.

Rowe and Kahn (1998), drawing upon earlier ideas such as activity theory (see Chapter 3), developed a theory of what they termed 'successful ageing', suggesting that the key to 'keeping active' in later life was social engagement, active exercise, proactive diet and avoiding disease. With this approach, maintaining the balance achieved in mid-life for as long as possible was seen as a desirable goal for healthy ageing.

Both approaches, however, raise difficulties for the period leading to the end of life. Gilleard and Higgs (2010) highlight the fact that past representations of old age as a period of sickness and infirmity stand in marked contrast to contemporary notions of 'active ageing'. Indeed, in some respects, the pressures facing 'very elderly' people may have become even more difficult given the popularity of suggestions that tangible or overt signs of ageing need to be resisted or held at bay for as long as possible (Binstock and Fishman, 2010). In contrast, Gilleard and Higgs (2010: 121) view the fourth age as a 'social space' which can be viewed as 'marking the end or collapse of "the third age project" where power, status and citizenship can no longer be enacted by those who are identified by it'. The contrast here is with the emergence of a 'third age' emphasizing choice and autonomy, and a 'fourth age' where the individual surrenders control to the frailties and indignities of late old age.

Grenier (2012: 174), however, questions the basis of an approach which treats the third age as a period of freedom and choice and were the fourth age is characterized solely by decline and dependency:

> The concern is that in recognising the fourth age as characterised solely by impairment, older people in this category become socially and culturally 'othered' – both from society and within groups of older people. This is especially the case if the 'accepted' construct privileges social and cultural notions of decline and devalues other subjective meanings, and the emotional significance of this change.

From a sociological perspective, the distinction between the different experiences of ageing – autonomy on the one side and fear of losing control on the other – is amplified through processes associated with individualization and the fragmentation of social institutions. The resulting tension is between the arrival of population ageing as a social phenomenon requiring a collective response, and the contrasting move towards individualizing social needs. Bauman (2000: 37–8) summarizes this development as follows:

> Individualization is here to stay; all thinking about the means of dealing with its impact in the fashion in which we all conduct our lives must start from acknowledging this fact. Individualization brings to the ever-growing number of men and women an unprecedented freedom of experimenting – but . . . it also brings the unprecedented task of coping with their consequences. The yawning gap between the right of self-assertion and the capacity to control the social settings which render such self-assertion feasible or unrealistic seems to be the main contradiction of [contemporary] modernity.

Elsewhere, Bauman (2000: 34) notes: 'Risks and contradictions go on being socially produced; it is just the duty and the necessity to cope with them which are being individualized.' Linked with this is another aspect of modernity, which Giddens (1991) defines as the 'sequestration of experience', identified as the separation of day-to-day life from contact with experiences which raise potentially disturbing existential questions – especially those associated with ageing and death. Essentially, these become detached from social and communal influences, emerging as a 'trajectory which relates above all to the individual's projects and plans'. Social ties (notably family and friends) may of course continue to influence the shaping and development of such plans. Nonetheless, the focus is upon how individuals manage the direction of their own ageing; in particular, how to stay in control for as long as possible through the third and fourth ages.

The medicalization of ageing

The individualizing processes which are transforming ageing run parallel with another set of social processes equally influential in the construction of later life. While the individual has responsibility for managing ageing, detailed knowledge about the processes involved are now transmitted (and validated) through the medical profession. Vincent (2003: 138) observes how 'the treatment of old age within a framework of medical knowledge gave doctors unrivalled social esteem and professional power'. Science came to be viewed – and especially the biomedical sciences – as the dominant medium through which many of the problems and challenges of ageing could be solved. This development led to a number of important characteristics in the way responses to ageing developed from the mid-twentieth century.

First, there was what Estes and Binney (1989: 587) were to describe as the 'biomedicalization of ageing', which has two central features: '(1) the social construction of ageing as a medical problem (thinking of ageing as a medical problem), and (2) the praxis (or practice) of ageing as a medical problem'. The approach adopted by the biomedical model was to view the ageing process as characterized by various processes of decline and decay. Estes and Binney summarized this perspective as one that saw old age as a medical problem that could be alleviated, if not eradicated, through the 'magic bullets' of medical science. The focus was on individual organic pathology and medical interventions, with physicians placed in charge of the definition and treatment of old age as a disease.

Following on from the above has been the crucial role of the pharmaceutical industry in determining appropriate responses to the 'problem' of ageing populations. The expansion of the industry was driven by demographic change, even though older people have often been excluded from clinical trials for new drugs (Bartlam et al., 2010). In the post-war era, effective medicines multiplied at an unparalleled rate in countries across Western Europe (Burns and Phillipson, 1986). Underpinning the drugs boom was the demand for tranquillizers (from the mid-1960s onwards), anti-hypertensives (from the mid- to late 1960s), and non-steroidal anti-inflammatory drugs (NSAIDs) (from the mid-1970s). In the UK, prescription items per head for older people nearly doubled over the period from 1997 to 2007 – from 22.3 to 42.4 (equivalent figures for those aged 16–59/64 were 6.3 and 9.5). The bulk of prescription items dispensed by community pharmacists and dispensing doctors are for older people (68 per cent) (Office for National Statistics [ONS], 2008c). Much of older people's increased use of medication reflects the greater prevalence of disabling conditions such as cancer, diabetes and musculoskeletal problems associated with arthritis and rheumatism. However, the limitations of alternatives have also played a part. Three factors in particular might be singled out: first, the marginal role of health promotion and preventative approaches in tackling conditions associated with ageing; second, restrictions on community and residential care both financially and in respect of the marginalization of social as opposed to medical models of care; third, older people's own limited knowledge – or, more accurately, fears and anxieties about ageing – which increased reliance upon different combinations of drug treatment.

A further issue concerns the way in which biomedicalization has interpreted both changes to the body in late life and the threat of cognitive decline. On the first of these, Katz (2010) notes how, despite the growth of interest in the sociology of the body (e.g. Shilling, 2008; Turner, 2008), the issue of the ageing body has received much less attention. Katz suggests that the biological realities of ageing are often placed outside the purview of social inquiry, resulting in a paradoxical position:

> [W]hile the ageing body is absent from most gerontological and sociocultural conceptions of the ageing process, the body is everywhere in social representations of the ageing process, embedded in all the surfaces and identities of ageing individuals' cultural and moral worlds. This is the paradox at the heart of social [investigations into ageing], whereby the body becomes the target of the overlapping resistance to and denial of ageing. (2010: 358)

Sociological perspectives provide an important corrective to biomedical approaches by demonstrating the impact of changes to the body on self-identity and self-esteem. Bury (1991) highlights the extent to which many of the long-term illnesses experienced by older people (including disabling conditions such as arthritis) can lead to a progressive loss of confidence in the body. This may serve to undermine relationships in old age, including those with family and friends.

Sociological perspectives also highlight the damage caused by making bodies invisible in the environments in which care takes place (see further below). Twigg's (2000, 2006) research illustrates this point highlighting how care-work of the ageing body (in residential homes and hospitals) tends to be thought of as dirty and demeaning, with older people themselves often viewing their own bodies as unclean. This finding also links with what Katz (2010: 358) sees as the broader 'disparagement of ageing' within contemporary society and the valorization of individuals who demonstrate 'resistance' to or 'reversal' of the ageing process (see further, Binstock and Fishman, 2010).

In the second area, that of cognitive impairment, sociological approaches have again been subordinate to a dominant biomedical model. Fears about ageing are especially focused on changes associated with brain functioning and, in particular, the possibility of experiencing a form of dementia known as Alzheimer's disease (AD). In the UK, the number of people with AD is projected to rise to over one million by 2021, including one in three of those aged 85 and over and one in two of those aged 95 and over. Worldwide, by 2021 dementia is likely to affect around 30 million people, with this number rising exponentially as life expectancy continues to increase across low- as well as high-income countries. Yet despite the widespread application of the Alzheimer's label as referring to the most common cause of dementia, there is no common agreement either on the nature of the disease or on how it should be diagnosed. George and Whitehouse (2010: 347) note that AD is sometimes known as a 'diagnosis of exclusion', 'since no direct proof of its presence can be obtained and 25 or more other diagnoses for cognitive deficits must be ruled out'. The research and treatment response to AD has, however, been predominantly at the biomedical level, with the search to uncover alterations to DNA and subsequent changes in proteins which influence brain functioning. Yet George and Whitehouse (2010) question just how helpful the molecular-genetic paradigm is likely to be, given that Alzheimer's is a condition influenced by a variety of environmental and lifestyle factors operating throughout the life course. They go on to argue:

> Although our molecular genetic comprehension of Alzheimer's disease is still nebulous, what is clear is that powerful social forces such as government organizations and the pharmaceutical industry have promoted the molecular movement

in Alzheimer's for the past several decades, and in doing so, endorsed a story that has misled the public with promises for a cure, while directing attention away from likely social causes and more fundamental issues of inclusion and community response. (2010: 348)

An additional step in their argument – one which raises fundamental issues for our treatment of people diagnosed or suspected of having Alzheimer's – is that the 'disease' label itself stigmatizes those to whom it is applied. People with dementia, as Kitwood (1997: 14) argued in his pioneering work, are turned into a 'different species' and presented as less than human, entering 'a second childhood' or 'experiencing a living death' (George and Whitehouse, 2010; see also Gubrium, 1986). Douthit (2006: 170) argues that the difficulty with the biomedical and neurodegenerative focus is that it 'fails to capture the profound sense of anxiety, grief, sadness, loss of self-esteem, and need for relatedness experienced by Alzheimer's disease victims'. She concludes:

The disproportionate focus of drug and behavioural therapies on the cognitively misguided equates cognition with the totality of human essence. The loss of cognition and its attendant loss of a historical self-identity are mistakenly equated with the loss of a relational self. Afflicted elderly, suffering unspeakable losses, are thus objectified as an infantilized and disabled 'other' . . . For older persons needing to name their subjective experience and to find comfort in human relationships a meagre solace is salvaged from a hard-edged practice of mental health that embraces efficient, instrumental biologically-informed solutions and behavioural manipulations. (2006: 172–3)

One response to the above has been the emergence of a variety of perspectives which focus attention on the person rather than the disease. Kitwood (1997) developed this approach in the 1980s, with his emphasis on the role of personality in dementia alongside the influence of biographical factors and physical health. Subsequent developments have emphasized advocacy and self-help among people with dementia (Downs and Bowers, 2008), the application of narrative and biographical approaches (Basting, 2001), and validation and related therapies (Ray and Phillips, 2012).

However, the major thrust of research and treatment remains dominated by biomedical approaches which 'emphasize the negative aspects of growing older and militarize brain aging as a disease to be defeated' (George and Whitehouse, 2010: 353).

The marginalization of social models of care and broader sociological perspectives on issues relating to mental and physical changes affecting older people are borne out in the daily practice of health and social care. Here, fear and anxieties about ageing appear reinforced by social interactions within residential homes and hospitals, these often underlining a sense of the 'fourth age' as a period of loss of dignity and lack of control over daily life. Powerful evidence for this came in a variety of reports published in the early 2000s, and it is to a consideration of these that we now turn.

Ageing without dignity

In 2011 the Parliamentary Health Service Ombudsman for England published a report of an investigation into the treatment of 10 older people in NHS hospitals. The case studies, according to the report, demonstrated a 'picture of NHS provision . . . failing to meet even the most basic standard of care' (Parliamentary and Health Service Ombudsman [PHSO], 2011). These were not, it was pointed out in the report, 'exceptional or isolated cases'. Indeed, of the 'nearly 9,000 properly made complaints [to the Health Service Ombudsman in 2010], 18 per cent were about the care of older people' (PHSO, 2011: 8). The cases indicated the failure of services 'to look beyond a patient's clinical condition and respond to the social and emotional needs of the individual and their family' (PHSO, 2011: 8). To illustrate this point, the Ombudsman reported:

> Half the people featured in this report did not consume adequate food or water during their time in hospital . . . Carers or members of the family who might wish to help the patient eat and drink are not permitted to do so, and help with eating is not forthcoming from nursing staff . . . Old people are left in soiled or dirty clothes and are not washed or bathed. One

woman told us that her aunt was taken on a long journey to a care home by ambulance. She arrived strapped to a stretcher and soaked with urine, dressed in unfamiliar clothing held up by paper clips, accompanied by bags of dirty laundry, much of which was not her own. Underlying such acts of carelessness and neglect is a casual indifference to the dignity and welfare of older persons. (PHSO, 2011: 10)

The observations from the Health Service Ombudsman have been confirmed in a variety of reports about the care of older people. A Care Quality Commission survey published in 2009 found that one in five hospital patients who had difficulty feeding themselves (mostly older people) did not get help with meals (Care Quality Commission [CQC], 2009). This finding was reinforced in the findings from the CQC inspections of 100 NHS hospitals in England, which included an assessment of care standards for meeting nutritional needs. In all, 17 hospitals out of the 100 were failing to deliver care that met this standard. Some of the observations made in the report included: 'Patients were not given the help they needed to eat, meaning they struggled to eat or were physically unable to eat meals'; 'Patients were interrupted during meals and had to leave their food unfinished'; and 'Many patients were not able to clean their hands before meals' (CQC, 2011a: 15).

A report on hospital care of older people with dementia (also in 2009) found 54 per cent of their carers expressing the view that being in hospital had had a significant negative effect on the symptoms of dementia, with higher levels of confusion and reduced independence; 77 per cent of carer respondents were dissatisfied with the quality of care provided; 36 per cent of carers said the person with dementia was never treated with respect or dignity during their stay in hospital. Equally telling, and important in the context of the issue of the relationship between body image and self-esteem (see above), 60 per cent of carers were dissatisfied with standards of personal hygiene, and a similar figure for meeting continence needs (Alzheimer's Society, 2009). Problems in the care of people with dementia in hospital were born out by the National Audit of Dementia Care in General Hospitals (Royal College of Psychiatrists, 2011) which examined the extent to which people were receiving an adequate standard of care. The audit found 'a low level of performance' on key standards of care (e.g. in areas such as assessment and nutrition), with wide variation between the participating hospitals.

Poor standards of care have also been reported for the 400,000 older people (in the UK) in the residential and nursing home sector, with inspections in 2011 by the CQC rating one in seven residential homes as 'poor' or 'adequate'. Even more telling are figures for the large numbers of older people dying in care homes from conditions linked with poor standards of care and, in some cases, neglect. An analysis by the ONS of death certificates of care home residents in England and Wales over the period 2005–9 found 667 deaths due to dehydration, 157 to malnutrition, 579 to drug-resistant bacterium; 1,446 to pressure sores and 4,866 to septicaemia (cited in the *Independent*, 31 January 2011). Of course, many of those affected would have entered residential care in a debilitated state, either malnourished and/or in a poor state of physical health. Yet given the financial pressures on care homes arising from the shortfall in public funding, reductions on budgets for items such as food may give limited scope for assisting residents. One study of 53 homes (covering 1,747 places) in Sefton, Merseyside, carried out by Laing and Buisson in 2011, found an average of £27.50 a week spent on food per person, or £3.93 per day (one home was identified as spending as little as £2.27 a day for each resident) (cited in *The Sunday Times*, 12 February 2012). With sums of money as low as these, it is difficult to see how strategies to assist malnourished older people are likely to be put in place; more generally, the figures point to the limited choice which appears to exist in a basic area of daily living. The problems facing people in residential and nursing home care may be compounded by limited access to the full range of health and social care. This was highlighted in a 2010 survey of Primary Care Trusts (PCTs) conducted by the CQC, the subject of secondary analysis by the British Geriatric Society (CQC, 2012). This found a lack of consensus among PCTs in their commissioning role in terms of the provision of services to the residential sector. The survey suggested that only in 43 per cent of PCTs were older people likely to be getting access to all the services they required.

In terms of other areas of care, the 2010 *National Confidential Enquiry into Patient Outcome and Death* (NCEPOD) found that two out of three older patients admitted for emergency surgery received poor care, with many left in pain. This report also noted: 'Malnutrition is common in elderly surgical admissions, but documentation, nutritional assessment and evidence of appropriate management within this group was extremely poor.' For some diseases, older people receive less investigation and treatment in comparison with younger age groups. Foot and Harrison (2011) examined the evidence for different types of cancer and found that proportionately fewer older patients than younger patients received extensive surgery to remove tumours. They estimate that around 15,000 people in the UK over the age of 75 are dying prematurely from cancer each year when compared with the best performing countries.

The above reports highlight some of the issues facing people in late old age entering the care system. Of course, many older people do receive a dignified and supportive service which fully acknowledges the vulnerabilities which this period of life can bring. Yet the fact that many do not is reflected in the need for investigations such as those carried out by the Commission on Dignity in Care for Older People (CDCOP) (2012) established in response to the numerous reports identifying failings within the care system in respect of support for older people. The Commission argues that poor care is rooted in wider problems of age discrimination, which it sees as the 'most common form of discrimination in the UK':

> Increased life expectancy is a positive development but our view of older people focuses almost exclusively on biological decline, and we tend to discuss older people as a problem for health and social care services, a 'population time-bomb' or crisis we cannot afford. In contrast, the economic and social contribution offered by older people, for instance in employment, volunteering or caring for partners, children and other family members, is rarely acknowledged. (CDCOP, 2012: 7)

Marginalizing social care

But the extent to which these difficulties are embedded in issues concerning the balance between health and social care support and broader issues about social integration in late old age is important to acknowledge. Problems of care fundamentally concern old age: 70 per cent of acute hospital beds are occupied by older people, 20 per cent by people with dementia and 75 per cent of residents of care homes have dementia. Care is increasingly focused on end of life and, as argued above, is built around the attitudes and expectations we have about this period.

Yet three aspects are striking about the type of support received in old age. First, in terms of the balance between health and social care, expenditure is heavily weighted towards the former. The Dilnot Commission (2011) put the figures (for England) at £50 billion for the NHS compared with £8 billion spent on social care. This disparity does much to explain the dominance of medical models of care, further reinforced by views that the type of conditions that increasingly affect older people (such as dementia) are best understood within a biological-genetic paradigm.

Second, support within the social care system has itself been substantially reduced. In 2005 half of local authorities provided support to people assessed as having 'moderate' needs; by 2008 that figure had fallen to 18 per cent (Age UK, 2011). By 2016 it is likely that around one million older people needing care within the home will receive no formal support from public or private sector agencies. The reality is that reductions to public funding will have the greatest impact on low-income pensioners. They are unlikely to receive much in the way of preventative community care and funding permits only the shortest stay in residential care. Without any major reform in the health and social care system, experiences in late age will be stratified as much by income and social class as by the type of health or social difficulties affecting the elderly person.

Third, problems of delivering care to older people are exacerbated by the lack of integration between health and social care, with the House of Commons Health Committee (2012: 37) suggesting that little has been achieved despite attempts stretching over some 40 years and that progress 'continues to be disappointing'. The concern must be that integration, important though this may be, will come at the expense of further marginalizing social dimensions of care given the continued bias in spending towards expenditure on healthcare (from 2004 to 2009, net spending on social care for older people rose by 0.1 per cent per annum in real terms – a total of £43 million – compared to a 5 per cent rise in spending on the NHS – £25 billion – over the same period [King's Fund, 2009]).

All these factors have raised problems for handling the transitions which follow the onset of impairment in late old age. Grenier (2012) points to the complex subjective changes associated with long-term disabilities and illnesses, and the struggle which people have to maintain continuity with their past lives while recognizing the profound changes which physical and/or mental ill-health can bring. Crucially, Grenier (2012: 182) argues:

> With the dominant transition of work to retirement portrayed as one involving freedom, activity and leisure, and continuity predominantly focused on individual lifestyles, more difficult transitions – such as the acquisition of impairment in late life – remain unacknowledged. There is no space attributed to the more difficult transitional experiences; older people are left on their own to negotiate these changes.

This last point is central to the crisis of social ageing at the end of life. Much care, to reiterate an earlier observation, does strive to recognize and support the vulnerabilities and losses associated with late old age. But the individualization of the transition – notwithstanding the support of family and friends where these exist – places both acute pressures on the older individual as well as major responsibilities on the agencies and professionals involved. This highlights the particular challenge associated with ageing populations and the need to rethink many aspects of the social and economic institutions working on their behalf. This is a theme to which we shall return in the final two chapters of this book.

Conclusion: The contingencies of ageing

Conditions in the twenty-first century appear to have resurrected ageing – and late old age especially – as a time of fear and anxiety. Despite the care and support which people receive, the 'unknowns' crowd out many of the things to which people might look forward. 'End of life' remains uncertain territory, with the possibility of an incapacitating physical and/or mental condition, and the likelihood of death itself taking place in an unfamiliar space (almost certainly a hospital). Older people do now have – certainly in western society compared with any other historical period – greater choice and control over their lives, and this reflects the improvements to health and financial resources which took place over the course of the twentieth century. But, as Settersten and Trauten (2009: 457) point out: 'Being able to count on old age . . . is not the same as being able to predict *how* those years will be experienced or *whether* the balance of experiences will be positive.' They continue:

> [O]ne of the primary ways in which old age today is distinct from younger life periods is that *the later years have a highly contingent quality*. The fact that old age is longer and highly variable seems to have made its contingent quality more salient. Old age is embodied with so much possibility – yet its potentials, if they are to be realized, depend on some big 'ifs' that cannot be predicted or controlled . . . These . . . relate to life, health and resources: *if* I am (or we are) healthy, *if* I (or we) can manage financially, *if* I (or we) can live independently, *if* my (or our) children are able or willing to help, and so on. As these contingencies come undone, so too do the futures that have been counted on or taken for granted.

And, as the authors observe, how these big 'ifs' play out will depend on all the factors which sociologists use to understand the impact of social differences and social inequalities at other stages of the life course: notably, factors such as social class, ethnicity and gender. We might still want to pose the questions: Can we, as we move through the twenty-first century, make growing old *less* contingent and variable? Can we be more alive to its possibilities rather than its problems? Can we do more to embrace rather than exclude the changes it brings? We turn to these questions in the final part of this book.

Part III
New Pathways for Later Life

9
Preparing for Ageing Populations: Rebuilding Institutions

Introduction

The previous chapter highlighted the contingencies surrounding later life in the twenty-first century. For those of us in high-income countries, at least, we know for sure that it is more than likely that we will reach the period defined as 'old age'. People are viewed as 'unlucky' if they die in their 60s and even early 70s. Increasingly, achieving the age of 80 or even 90 is coming to be expected. To be sure, class variations (as highlighted in Chapter 2) in life expectancy remain hugely significant and look set to remain so given the toll of economic recession and rise in long-term unemployment. But the reality of a long life is now deeply embedded in western society and is becoming increasingly common across all societies of the world. Yet what to do with these extra years and how to integrate them into the whole life course are major questions that have to be addressed. There is much discussion about the need to develop 'active ageing' (World Health Organization, 2001), 'intergenerational solidarity' (European Commission, 2009) and 'building a society for all ages' (Department for Work and Pensions, 2009). But the mechanisms for achieving these aspirations are unclear, as are the resources which might be available to deliver such goals.

The purpose of this chapter is to consider some of the dilemmas which confront the need to rebuild and reconnect with ageing populations. The first part of the chapter identifies some of the reasons behind the current difficulties facing these societies at the present time. In the second part, the discussion moves to identifying particular challenges, focused on the debate around extending working lives and lifelong learning. The review of these areas provides a framework for the final chapter of the book which develops the theme of ageing populations as forming the basis for a new ethic of interdependent and cooperative relationships.

Understanding ageing: Integration or segregation?

Ageing populations cannot be described as a new challenge for our social and economic institutions – at least not for western governments. France became aware of the impact of declines in fertility as early as the eighteenth century and was expressing fears about the consequences of ageing populations in the nineteenth – notably around the possibility of a shortage of conscripts for its army. The UK replayed such anxieties at different times through the twentieth century, notably after the Second World War, as illustrated in the 1949 Royal Commission on Population. This voiced apprehension over rising levels of consumption by elderly people, who 'consume without producing', thus 'reducing the average standard of life for [all] generations' (Royal Commission on Population, 1949: 322). Such views softened over succeeding decades but were taken up again in the 1970s and 1980s with the 'worker versus pensioner' debate (Johnson et al., 1989) and have reappeared in the twenty-first century with anxieties about the economic and political impact of a 'large' baby-boom generation (Willetts, 2010; see also Chapter 2).

But if the challenge and anxieties associated with ageing are not new, neither is their underlying cause: namely how to 'integrate' such populations with other age and social groups. The tension here is between viewing 'late life' or 'old age' as a distinctive stage with its own rights, needs and obligations and that which places it within the context of the life course as a whole (Grenier, 2012). As has been argued elsewhere in this book, the former approach has tended to dominate thinking about ageing, notably with the formation of institutions – such as retirement and the welfare state – which placed older people into defined categories with particular needs. This secured 'integration' to a degree, but at a price to the individual – that of 'structured dependency' (Townsend, 1981) at best; at worst, exclusion from many of the institutions and activities which pass for normal living (Baars, 2012; Scharf et al., 2002).

But if 'integration' through what came to be known as the 'three boxes' of education, work and retirement has itself now been weakened (with the demise of 'traditional' retirement along with the welfare state), the alternatives are themselves equally unclear. Moody (1988: 28–9) developed this point when he referred to the condition of ageing reflecting 'the . . . contradictory experience of modernity' – i.e. old age – as 'both loss of meaning and greater opportunity for freedom'. Moody suggests:

> It is not simply that 'modernization' has weakened or transformed the status of the elderly or thrown previous values into question. More strikingly, old age itself, as a period of life, is no longer felt merely as a climax, brief or extended, to earlier habits of life. The enlarged time period of old age itself incorporates . . . the contradictions of modernity. Modern societies create economic and technological conditions that vastly enlarge the abundance of life for an ever larger segment of the population. But this abundance of life is increasingly felt as a void . . . Old age, like modernity itself, is the simultaneous experience of emptiness and fullness. It is the emptying of fixed values and the fullness of possibilities.

The search for new forms of integration has found expression in different ways. A common approach has been to focus on the development of a 'third age', where the potential of ageing is realized through lifestyles built around new forms of consumption (Gilleard and Higgs, 2005). This period is differentiated from a 'fourth age', where the possibilities of active lifestyles recede as individuals cope with the challenges associated with chronic and disabling illnesses. Another approach is to resist any change associated with ageing. This perspective – known as 'productive' or 'successful' ageing (see Chapter 3) – is reflected in Mayer's (2011: 9) description of the rise of 'amortality', defined as the 'increasing trend to live the same way throughout life, however that life is lived, and for as long as possible'.

Approaches associated with the 'third age' or 'successful' ageing do not themselves resolve the social challenges associated with population change. Indeed, they continue to pitch the solutions largely at an individual level – i.e., ageing as a 'personal' rather than a 'collective' responsibility. Moreover, the problem of what Baars (2012) views as an 'anti-ageing culture' becomes even more embedded within social and economic institutions. Wider anxieties about failing economies are increasingly displaced onto the shoulders of ageing populations where the so-called 'spiralling' costs associated with pensions and healthcare are seen as dragging down the prospects for society as a whole (Howker and Malik, 2010).

The debate about ageing suffers from a more deep-seated flaw – one to which the academic disciplines have themselves in part contributed. The simple confusion here is between the issue of individual ageing – where some element of decline and death is inevitable – and population ageing – where new opportunities are introduced with the collective expansion of the human life course. The discussion about ageing as a social and cultural phenomenon often seems simply to project ageing at an individual level onto the fate of institutions themselves. This is to miss the point that institutions of all kinds – family, work, educational, leisure – can create new opportunities from the development of ageing populations. Moody (2010: 16) argues:

> Instead of treating the life course as fixed, in the future we may come to see later life as a period more susceptible to intervention and improvement. Instead of viewing ageing only as decline, it is possible to provide incentives that modify the lifestyles and behaviours of older people. The goal would be to move from an age-differentiated society to an age-integrated society, where opportunities in education, work and leisure are open to people of every age.

It is clearly the case that there is a great deal of work to be done in respect of achieving the desirable goal of 'age integration'. The paradox of contemporary society is that while much is made of the need to involve older people in areas such as work and education, these institutions 'disengage' from people at a particular chronological point. The next part of this chapter reviews some of the evidence in relation to employment and education as well as setting out some alternative approaches.

Extending working life: Myths and realities

The policy of extending working lives has been a significant outcome of the debate concerning the economic sustainability of ageing populations, and reflects in large measure many concerns identified above. In essence, the discussion has shifted from focusing upon *early retirement/early exit* to identifying *pathways into work or maintaining older people in employment*, with particular encouragement given to work beyond state pension age (SPA). The aim is to reverse the trend, characteristic of the 1980s and 1990s, whereby large numbers of older workers left work ahead of SPA, and where early retirement came to be accepted as a normal event in the life course. Increasingly, governments are aiming to adjust pension ages in line with increases in longevity – in effect, forcing people to stay in employment well into their 60s and potentially into their 70s. Yet this policy shift has come with no corresponding policy concerning how work environments might support older workers or whether appropriate jobs will be available (Phillipson and Smith, 2005).

Training in the workplace would, at first sight, appear to be a priority given the focus on retaining older workers in employment. In reality, however, this area has suffered considerable neglect over the years – despite attempts in public policy to emphasize the value of older employees. The benefit of training and learning, across all age groups, appears to be widely acknowledged. The Department for Education and Skills (2005: §210) argued that there was good evidence that 'older people can benefit substantially from continuing to learn and gain new skills'. Given a policy of extending the period of employment, the expectation must be that older workers will have an equal opportunity with younger age groups of sharing in different types of training and learning. The reality, however, based on a range of surveys in the UK and elsewhere, would suggest that this is invariably the exception rather than the rule. A benchmark survey of factors influencing older workers' participation in employment highlighted evidence for the sharp age-related decline in training (Humphrey et al., 2003). Of particular note was the extent to which encouragement from employers to learn new skills underwent a significant decline after the age of 55 – notably so in the case of men. Over half of male employees (56 per cent) reported little or no encouragement to learn more job-related skills, compared with 44 per cent of those aged 50–54; corresponding figures for women were 44 and 37 per cent.

Lissenburgh and Smeaton's (2003) analysis of Labour Force Survey (LFS) data confirmed the link between increased age and declining access to training. Logistic regression models used in their study suggested that men and women in part-time and temporary employment were especially disadvantaged in respect of training. Humphrey et al. (2003) also found that the level of encouragement to undertake training varied between full- and part-time employees. In their survey one-third of part-time employees were offered no encouragement to learn more job-related skills, compared with one-quarter of full-time employees. Such findings are especially important given the growth of 'non-standard' forms of work, such as part-time and casual working. Over time, this will almost certainly lead to an increase in people denied access to training in the workplace.

Data from the LFS confirm the link between participation in training and socioeconomic status. Analysis of the 2008 survey found that 35 per cent of those in professional occupations had received training in the three months preceding the interview compared with 13 per cent of those in routine occupations (Schuller and Watson, 2009). The occupational sector in which the individual works also appears to be influential. Schuller and Watson (2009: 69) highlight the fact that working in the public sector significantly increases the chances of accessing some form of training. Over 40 per cent of those who received some form of training in the three months prior to the interview, and who had been in employment from the age of 25 to retirement, had worked in the public sector; 21 per cent had worked in the private sector. Given the projected decline in public sector employment, this is a highly significant contrast, which will have potentially serious consequences for access to training for older workers and other groups.

Newton et al. (2005) reported on the availability of training among the unemployed and economically inactive. This study shows that, overall, fewer than 1 in 10 report involvement in training and that training participation declines rapidly with age. The likelihood of someone aged 55 and over participating in training is 50 per cent less compared with an adult aged 35–44. McNair et al. (2004) found that levels of support given to those changing their job declined with age. Older workers were less likely than younger ones to receive any help during a job transition (37 per cent of older workers, against 47 per cent of those under 50). They were less likely to receive training from their employers, help from their workmates and colleagues, or support from a government agency. They were also more likely to have sought support for themselves, either through the internet or via other informal sources.

At the same time, it is important to recognize contradictory signs in the evidence for participation in training. Smeaton and McKay (2003) make the point that many older workers remain committed to career development. In their survey, 33 per cent of 60–64-year-olds had undertaken training at some point in the previous three years. Cheung and Mckay (2010) noted some positive developments in participation trends, examining evidence from the LFS over the period 1994–2008. Although they confirmed that training remained least common for the over-60s, participation had in fact increased over the period studied. The authors suggest that this 'may be a positive sign that older workers are receiving opportunities that perhaps were [previously] more concentrated on younger workers' (2010: 38).

There is some evidence that workers may themselves show resistance to the idea of further training. This may happen where they lack confidence about learning new skills (Newton et al., 2003) or because they feel that acquiring them is unnecessary or may go unrewarded (McNair and Flynn, 2005). Taylor and Urwin's (2001) research conducted in the late 1990s suggested that declining participation in training was linked to employer decision-making rather than individual preference not to undertake training. Urwin (2004: 28), on the other hand, argues that not only is training less likely to be offered to older individuals, but also that 'large proportions of this group have not taken up the opportunity to train'. Information on this issue is provided by Felstead (2010) in research covering the employment experiences of workers in the UK aged 20–65. Findings from the 2006 Skills Survey used in the study indicated that around two-thirds of men and women aged 50–65 said they 'did not want any training' compared with between one-third and two-fifths of younger workers. Older workers not in receipt of training also rated its benefits lower when compared with younger workers. Interestingly, the evidence did not point to employers being reluctant to provide training to older workers. Indeed, the reverse appeared to be the case, with a slightly higher proportion of younger workers reporting a lack of willingness on the part of their employer to provide training when it was wanted (Felstead, 2010: 1310).

Employers are likely to vary considerably in their approach to training. McNair et al. (2004) found that people in large firms continued to develop skills in a way that was less true of those in small and medium-sized enterprises (SMEs). Some groups – notably those drawn from managerial and professional backgrounds – appear much more likely to support training than others (for example, those in elementary occupations). Level of skill and qualification (or human capital) appears critical – those with higher degrees and/or professional qualifications are more likely to participate in training later in their working life compared with those with lower-level qualifications (Newton et al., 2003). For professional/managerial groups, external pressure to extend working life may not be a major issue given that higher qualifications and socioeconomic class is a strong predictor of a longer working life (McNair et al., 2004). For some manual groups, however, deficits in training over the life course may be difficult to correct, especially given limited workplace opportunities and depressed expectations about learning (Schuller and Watson, 2009).

Against the above, largely negative, findings must be balanced more positive developments which may be important over the medium and longer term. Future generations of older workers can be expected to have higher levels of basic numeracy and literacy skills and this should have a major impact on participation in continuing education and training. Dixon (2003) notes from the LFS the strong relationship between level of qualification and the likelihood of undertaking job-related training, as well as the finding that those with higher existing qualifications are more likely to be studying for a new qualification. She concludes: 'These relationships suggest that age-specific differentials in learning activity could flatten in future as the fraction of older workers who have not completed secondary education gradually declines' (2003: 74). On the other hand, stimulation and encouragement from employers and line managers will be vital if opportunities for training and learning are to be realized. The workplace remains a vital source for gaining knowledge about learning opportunities: 50 per cent of people aged 45–54 found out about their current main learning activity through work (either their employer or workmates); the equivalent figure for those aged 55–64 was 30 per cent (Aldridge and Tuckett, 2007). These figures will need to be built upon given a policy of extending working life, with a fresh emphasis on developing training and learning within the work environment. The next section of this chapter examines some key policies which will need to be developed.

Policy initiatives to expand workplace training

The numerous changes affecting people aged more than 50 years suggests the need for innovation in a key area of public policy. Among these, access to training and education in the second half of the life course will be a crucial area for development, with significant implications for health and well-being in the workplace (Vickerstaff et al., 2011). Ford (2005) makes the point that although many of those aged 50-plus have skills and experience currently lost to the economy, learning requirements are higher than for younger age groups. One in three in this age group experience literacy or numeracy problems, as compared with one in five of those in their late 20s/early 30s. Mayhew and Rijkers (2004) stress the importance of 'continuous learning during the whole of working life as a means of reducing the dangers of labour market disadvantage in the older years'. Ford (2005: 10) makes the case for an 'overall national third age guidance and learning strategy', one which would be linked to the national skills strategy and which would enable adults from midlife onwards to maximize their skills and potential (see further Schuller and Watson, 2009). Assisting this will, however, require a reversal of current policies which are reducing public funding for adult learners, with the greatest felt by those in the 50-plus age group (Aldridge and Tuckett, 2007). Policies for change will need to focus on the following areas:

- developing entitlements for 'third age learning';
- reassessing methodologies and techniques for training older workers;
- expanding provision for those in non-standard forms of employment.

The first area has been addressed by Schuller and Watson (2009) as part of their inquiry into the future of lifelong learning. In their recommendations for change, they set out a four-stage model to encourage learning across the life course, recognizing different periods of development in the years up to 25, 25–49, 50–74 and 75-plus. They suggest that what has been termed the 'third age' (50–74) should be viewed as a central period for encouraging enhanced training and education opportunities, based upon a more even distribution of work across the life course. This would be buttressed by: (a) a fairer allocation of educational resources (public, private and employer-based) to meet the needs of third and fourth age (those aged 75-plus) groups; (b) a legal entitlement of free access to learning to acquire basic skills (e.g. in literacy and numeracy); (c) a 'good practice' entitlement to learning leave as an occupational benefit; (d) specific 'transition entitlements' – e.g. for people on their 50th birthday – to 'signal the continuing potential for learning of those moving into the third age' (Schuller and Watson, 2009: 133).

The second area concerns methodologies for training older workers. This raises issues about developing more effective training programmes targeted at older adults. The research evidence reviewed above suggests that employer (or line manager) 'discouragement' partly explains decreasing participation in training. Yet this is not a complete explanation of the problem. In particular, workers themselves may consider – after a certain age or stage in their career – that further training is unnecessary. Or, as is also possible, they may feel that the type of training and learning they are likely to receive is inappropriate given their level of skill and experience. Czaja and Sharit (2009: 266) make the point that although many existing training techniques are effective for older adults, we lack an adequate research database to 'determine whether some training techniques are consistently differentially beneficial to older workers'.

On the other hand, literature from work-based psychological studies has demonstrated the benefits as well as the limitations of particular approaches to training involving older workers. Tsang (2009: 289), for example, cites a number of studies which show how relatively small amounts of training can reverse cognitive decline and assist the retention of newly acquired skills. Conversely, the limitations of training benefits are also noted, including reduced magnitude of learning and slower learning rates. Given the emergence of a more diverse ageing workforce, attention to new ways of delivering work-based training would seem to be an urgent requirement. One suggestion would be to encourage a single organization to lead research and policy initiatives linking trades unions, business organizations and government around the theme of training for an ageing workforce. This would require dedicated funding and staffing but could be part of an existing body. The Third Age Employment Network (TAEN) would be one possibility to take the lead in developing such an initiative.

The third area concerns the need to encourage training programmes specifically targeted at those in part-time and flexible forms of employment, and at those older workers who are self-employed. The issues here have been summarized by Czaja and Sharit (2009: 259) as follows:

> [A]s the number of workers in non-standard work arrangements . . . continues to increase, one important issue confronting workers will be access to traditional workplace benefits such as training. [Such] workers will be less likely to receive structured company-sponsored training and the responsibility of continuous learning and job training will fall to a greater extent on the individual. It is not yet clear how to best develop and disseminate training programs to promote lifelong learning for these 'non-traditional' workers. This issue is especially pertinent for older workers, given that they are less likely to be provided with access to training and development programmes in traditional work environments where company-sponsored training is available.

There are no easy solutions to the problems facing part-time and related groups of workers. On the one side, studies already cited (e.g. Lissenburgh and Smeaton, 2003; Humphrey et al., 2003) highlight inequalities between full and part-time workers in respect of access to training. Such difficulties are unlikely to have changed – they have probably worsened – in the period since the research was published. On the other side, opportunities from providers such as community and further education colleges have been steadily reduced, with the major focus now placed on preparing younger people for entry into the labour market. Some options for consideration here might include: first, adoption of Schuller and Watson's (2009) plan for a legal entitlement to learn through adult life (see above); second, more imaginative use of computer-based training or e-learning to assist those working from home or those juggling work and care-giving responsibilities (Czaja and Sharit, 2009); third, specific obligations placed upon employers to expand training and learning as a pre-condition for creating non-standard forms of employment.

But population ageing raises a significant challenge for another major social institution – higher education – one which at present (and especially in the UK) is largely disengaged from involvement with older people. It is to a consideration of the possibilities here that we now turn.

Responding to population ageing: Issues for higher education

Population ageing offers higher education institutions both challenges and opportunities. The twenty-first century will require societies, it is argued in this book, to find novel ways of managing demographic change, whether through encouraging new intergenerational ties, combining different forms of formal and informal support or facilitating a more even spread of work across the life course. In all these areas, education – and higher education in particular – could play a key role in helping institutions adapt: whether by encouraging new types of adult learning through all phases of the life course, training professionals who work with older people or creating new forms of civic engagement (Achenbaum, 2005).

Taking the UK as an example, what is known about the participation of older people – defined here as those aged 50 and over – in higher education? Published data in the UK in fact provides very little information on this age group. The Higher Education Statistics Agency (HESA) groups together mature and older learners in the category age 30 and above. Regular reports on the profile of universities, such as *Patterns of Higher Education Institutions in the UK* (Universities UK, 2010) do not provide separate figures for the 50-plus age group. Research from Phillipson and Ogg (2010) draws on data supplied by the HESA to provide a more detailed breakdown of older people on undergraduate and taught postgraduate, full- and part-time courses. The selected years are: 1998/99, 2002/03 and 2007/08. Full-time and sandwich/full-time students are those normally required to attend an institution for periods amounting to at least 24 weeks within the year of study. Part-time students are those recorded as studying part time, or studying full time on courses lasting less than 24 weeks, on block release, or studying during the evenings only.

The findings confirm the sharp drop after the age of 50 in the above modes of study. Full-time 50-plus students remain a tiny group within UK universities, with fewer than 4,000 first-year students on undergraduate and postgraduate courses in 2007/08 (an increase of around 1,400 from 1998/99).

Among part-time students, however, the 50-plus group are better represented, comprising 15 per cent of all first-year part-time undergraduates in 2007/08 (a similar proportion to that in 1998/99) and 10 per cent of first-year part-time postgraduates. This adds up to nearly 62,000 students across the UK (an increase of around 18,400 since 1998/99). Those aged 60 and over comprise 6 per cent of first-year students in the UK, a total of nearly 20,000 students (a slight fall in percentage terms since 1998/99). The 50-plus subdivide into three groups: first, those undertaking professional/vocational qualifications (sometimes supported by their employer); second, those taking non-vocational courses (for example, in adult and continuing education) – an important market for those aged 60 and over; third, those studying for a degree but preferring a part-time route for financial, work-related or other reasons.

The importance of part-time and distance learning is confirmed in studies of institutions specializing in such provision. Examples here include the Open University (OU) and Birkbeck College, where, in both cases, around 20 per cent of graduating students are aged 51 or above (Jamieson, 2007). Research by Feinstein et al. (2007) found the average age of graduates to be 43 at Birkbeck and 44 at the OU. Open University data on the type of modules for which people aged 50-plus register indicate a broad spread of interests across the arts, social sciences and natural sciences. However, students aged 50-plus tend to favour short courses (10–15 credits), notably in the arts, languages (summer schools in particular) and the natural sciences (including maths and computing).

Social class is also strongly linked to participation of older students within higher education. Jamieson's 2007 survey of students (aged 61 and above) from Birkbeck and the Open University confirmed that most were from senior or professional or managerial occupations. The Birkbeck group was already highly qualified on entry, with around one in five having a postgraduate qualification. The association between social class and continuing education is highlighted in the analysis by Jenkins (2011) of data from the English Longitudinal Study of Ageing. This showed that nearly one-third of those aged 50-plus with a degree had participated in music,

arts or evening classes in the 12 months preceding the interview, with about the same proportion having undertaken a
formal education or training course. In comparison, for those
with no qualification, fewer than 5 per cent had attended a
formal training course or been to an evening class in the
previous 12 months.

More information is needed on how institutional barriers
limit participation in education. There is some evidence that
adults have limited knowledge about entry requirements or
about what the cost of higher education might entail (Pollard
et al., 2008). We know that older learners' motivations for
learning are different from those of younger age groups. Personal interest in the subject and the enjoyment of learning
are, for example, more important than work-related benefits.
Pollard and colleagues (2008) found people in the 45–55 age
group inclined towards academic rather than vocational subjects; this linked with 'personal development' as the main
motivation for study. Jamieson's (2007) survey of Birkbeck
and OU students also ranked personal development and
'interest in subject' as an important reason for wanting to
study. On the other hand, Jamieson emphasizes the heterogeneity of the students, most of whom were using the educational system to make themselves more attractive to employers
or to help them change their type of work. This was more
the case with those in their 50s than those in their 60s. Dench
and Regan (2000) concluded from their study of people aged
50–71 (based on a sample drawn from the National Adult
Learners Survey) that the most important reasons for learning
were intellectual – for example, wanting to 'keep the brain
active', and enjoying the challenge of learning new things.
Instrumental reasons, such as having to do some learning for
work, appeared much less important.

Thus far, older learners remain largely outside formal education, with involvement in higher education going into sharp
decline after the age of 50. At the same time, the number of
older learners moving into higher education will almost certainly increase given broader demographic and social changes.
Key challenges here include: first, the entry into retirement
of the baby boom generation, a group with higher levels of
education and strong aspirations to engage in learning;
second, pressures to extend working life for economic,

financial as well as social reasons; third, changes around midlife and raised aspirations about goals for the second half of life.

The above factors are transforming the landscape for higher education and its relationship with older people. In the 1960s, despite the post-war evolution of youth as a social and economic category, higher education in the UK was focused on an elite category of students (around 6 per cent of the age group). Youth, in this context, had been constructed 'outside' rather than through the higher education system. Most people in the current 50-plus age group are 'outside' the university system, with 'later life' or the 'third age' developing as a category insulated from higher education. Many of the baby boomers will, however, have 'passed through' higher education and/or will have engaged with the system through supporting their children's university education.

More than three decades on, responding to a new group hitherto excluded from higher education poses a fresh challenge, but current policy is yet to take account of the reality that older people will be living longer and more actively. Investment now in education – and higher education in particular – could have major benefits for individuals and for society: first, by playing a leading role in creating a new type of ageing for the twenty-first century, built around extended economic, family and citizenship roles; second, by supporting people planning the two decades or more beyond their main work careers; third, by unlocking mental capital and promoting well-being in later life; fourth, by supporting a range of professional and voluntary groups working on behalf of older people.

Reflecting on the above, four pathways might be envisaged for higher education to follow, both to attract older learners and those involved as professionals with this group:

1 *Educational and personal development programmes*: these would build upon existing work in adult and continuing education, but would identify new types of courses and markets among a diverse and segmented post-50s market.
2 *Employment-related programmes*: these might support the policy objective of extending working life, although the

extent of employer-demand may be fragile in the context of high levels of unemployment. The development of courses supporting people moving from full-time paid employment to various forms of self-employment may, however, remain attractive.

3 *Social inclusion programmes*: substantial numbers of older people – in current as well as succeeding cohorts – remain educationally and socially disadvantaged. Higher education institutions, with partners such as local authorities, further education colleges and the major national charities, should focus on a 'widening participation' agenda that covers all age groups and not just the young and working adults.

4 *Health and social care programmes orientated to professionals working with older people*: programmes could vary from foundation degrees through to modules for continuing professional development, with the theme of maintaining 'active ageing' a key component.

Specific initiatives might include:

- piloting new undergraduate curriculum areas relevant to a cadre of service professionals working on behalf of older people: the demand for undergraduate programmes in gerontology is untested in the UK but is a major area in the US;
- developing modules on 'active ageing' as a component in professional training for health and social care professionals: this could be a core or 'elective' on undergraduate programmes and/or part of continuing professional development (CPD);
- outreach programmes targeted at older people, perhaps in partnership with further education colleges or as a dimension to new campus developments: encouraging new types of courses focusing on 'healthy ageing' could be a major contribution to meeting the demographic challenge;
- establishing centres/institutes for learning in retirement in geographical areas with substantial ageing populations which could be ventures linked with local health and wellbeing boards, further education colleges and local authorities: they could combine health promotion and education,

building on the existing adult education tradition but developing programmes appropriate to older people with an extended period of initial and higher education;

- developing educational programmes that support new forms of civic engagement in later life – for example, 'environmental citizenship' and legal studies in 'human rights and community action': these may be attractive to a baby boom generation that has pioneered developments in these areas over the life course;

- developing training programmes targeted at older workers that are co-funded by employers: this may be especially important given pressures to reduce training opportunities for workers during periods of economic recession;

- targeting the 50-plus self-employed group, many of whom will be career/job changers with specific training requirements;

- establishing partnerships with Age UK and other relevant voluntary organizations to develop educational programmes focused on tackling social exclusion in later life: exploring co-funding through government and other agencies – developing innovative programmes that attract a wider range of social groups should be a key strategy for educational policy;

- developing ageing as a niche area for academic development by combining teaching older adults with a research focus.

Embedding older learners within higher education does, however, suggest a number of critical challenges. The first of these concerns the question of managing an 'intergenerational' mix within academic programmes. Currently, mature students are a minority on most full-time undergraduate programmes but make up a larger proportion on part-time courses. Increasing age diversity – especially on undergraduate courses – would itself raise difficult issues, such as managing a wider range of learning styles and different attitudes to learning, and would require universities – through their learning development units – to consider the implications of teaching across a wider spread of age groups. The American Council on Education (2007: 22) makes the following point:

Programming concerns can further obstruct older adults' access to higher education, including whether to develop separate programmes for older adults and how to make use of technology. At the heart of these issues is the range of motivations and needs of the older adult population – and the resulting flexibility that higher education institutions must have to deliver everything from career transition courses to leisure classes.

A second challenge is getting research evidence about the benefits of learning in later life. It is often claimed that education will improve physical and mental health, assist personal development, expand the range of social activities, and improve employment options. Evidence for this remains, however, somewhat limited – a fact noted in one of the few detailed UK studies of the impact of learning in later life (Jenkins, 2011). Jenkins highlights the limited amount of research on the health and social benefits of adult learning among older people. More work is needed to assess how education might improve the quality of life in old age. If the benefits could be demonstrated, the case for major investment in attracting older students to higher education would be stronger. Demonstrating that education can improve the quality of late life will be valuable not only for older people but also in highlighting the potential role of higher education in transforming the quality of life in old age.

A third challenge concerns developing a higher education strategy for older learners, who are neglected in part because of the lack of any obvious policy framework addressing their interests. At present, they fall into an unsatisfactory policy gap between conventional 'widening participation' and mainstream recruitment strategies. Most widening participation is not directed at older learners, and most recruitment efforts are still focused on those aged 25 and below. Consideration should be given to the development of a higher education strategy for older learners, which would develop the case for recruiting them into higher education. This strategy would need to focus around at least four areas: (a) targeting numbers for recruiting older (50-plus) learners over specific time periods; (b) identifying priority groups that might be targeted

– for example, early or late baby boomers; (c) developing appropriate programme/curriculum areas; (d) identifying geographical areas (for example, those with large proportions of older people) that might be the initial focus for activity.

A fourth challenge concerns the urgent question of funding. A strategy for older learners requires funding that can encourage universities to recruit among this group, and can find new sources of financial support for older learners. At present, self-funding or employer-supported fees are the main sources for older learners. The self-funded stream will remain an important element, although more information is needed about the range of fees appropriate to particular groups within the older population. Employer support is under pressure in the present economic climate, and older workers may be the first to lose out. The majority of older learners register as part-time students, with most being ineligible for government-funded financial support. Callender and Heller (2009) argue for equal treatment of part-time and full-time students, giving the former loans and grant support equivalent to that of full-timers on a pro-rata basis. Moving in this direction would clearly provide a major stimulus to closing the gap between the participation of older and younger learners within higher education.

Conclusion

The examples drawn from training and higher education are used to illustrate the importance of thinking about how to redesign social institutions to take advantage of ageing populations. The present debate is limited to viewing ageing as a problem which will restrict the development of institutions, whether limiting creativity in the workplace or reducing the supply (because of declining fertility) of people entering higher education. In both cases, social structures – those associated with work and higher education – have remained the same, while the life course itself has been transformed. This 'structural lag', as Riley et al. (1994) termed it, was certainly a problem in the relatively early stages of population ageing and was masked somewhat by the rise of retirement and the welfare state in the previous century. But with the changes to both, 'structural lag' has taken on a degree of social pathology in its consequences for the individual and society. The challenge here is not just one of changing social institutions. We also need to think about changing the social relationships which characterize the societies in which we live. This, it will be argued, is the ultimate challenge posed by ageing populations, namely supporting the search for more interdependent and cooperative relationships. It is to a discussion of these issues that we turn in the final chapter of this book.

10
Conclusion: New Pathways for Later Life

Introduction

As we move further into the twenty-first century it seems increasingly clear that momentum has slowed in the task of building a society that values and nurtures the possibilities and potential of ageing. This would seem a surprising statement given the extent of activity – from bodies such as the European Union and World Health Organization – to promote issues relating to ageing and around intergenerational solidarity. But as important as the various initiatives might be, countervailing pressures appear equally strong – as has been demonstrated at different points in this book. Ageing continues to be viewed as a significant burden on western economies; with the onset of recession and long-term unemployment, demographic change is seen as an acute problem. This dimension reflects the extent to which the welfare state and supporting institutions failed to build a satisfactory identity for later life (an argument developed in the work of Peter Townsend),[1] with the consequences becoming especially marked given the uncertainty surrounding retirement and welfare in the twenty-first century. Indeed, the biggest omission of the past 50 years has been the failure to explore the potential gains of an ageing population for social institutions, notably in the release of new energies and capacity for civic engagement, support for family and community activities, and distinctive forms of work and education.

Of course, many of the above activities developed anyway, as numerous studies demonstrated (see, for example, Achenbaum, 2005; Moody, 2010). Indeed, research on social aspects of ageing has been dominated by studies of the extensive family life of older people, the essential part they play in grandparenting, the importance of volunteering, and their contribution to the expansion of cultural and leisure activities. But this reshaping of ageing – led by older people themselves – contrasts sharply with the inflexibility of social institutions towards these populations. The original expression of the reshaping was articulated in the 'three boxes' of education, work and retirement – an attempt to 'manage' the life course in a way which emphasized the importance of work as a dominant life interest, preserving retirement as a form of 'structured dependency' (to use Townsend's [1981] original term). The breaking apart of the 'three boxes', with the insecurities surrounding transitions into and out of work and uncertainties concerning the timing of retirement, has opened new possibilities for reshaping the life course. The crisis of ageing is essentially the failure both to take advantage of these and to continue to represent population ageing as contributing to economic and social instability.

The key question for this book comes back to the task set out in the introduction: namely, how can social science contribute in helping us to think about the possibilities and potential behind the development of ageing populations? This, it might be argued, is a major discussion which needs to be developed at all public levels, building on similar debates conducted in the past.[2] This concluding chapter will provide some pointers to the way in which a discussion might be pursued, exploring the idea that the benefits of population ageing will come through acknowledgement of new forms of solidarity emerging among older people, families and generations, and across different nation-states.

Recognizing new forms of solidarity

Mutual solidarities

Current thinking about ageing is a problem because of the lack of connections made between the social changes that accompany ageing populations and the potential of these to transform the institutions in which ageing itself takes place. The idea that institutions are somehow 'damaged' by population ageing does indeed have wide currency – i.e., that 'dependency ratios' will rise, that costs (for health and social care) will increase and that certain conditions (such as dementia) will inflict a particular toll on carers and their families. A social science view on these issues might develop contrasting observations. In the first place, population ageing might itself provide a counterweight to negative aspects of modern society, such as the drift towards fragmentation and division within human relationships. Sennett (2012) illustrates the latter when he talks about the 'deskilling' now occurring in the social realm, matching that which took place within the workplace in the nineteenth and early twentieth centuries. He suggests that people are losing the skills to deal with intractable differences given the pressures generated by material inequality and the superficial nature of contacts within the workplace. Sennett concludes: 'We are losing the skills of co-operation to make a complex society work' (2012: 9).

Sennett's argument is that developing new forms of solidarity is essential given the complexity and diversity of modern societies. In this area, population ageing may in fact have much to offer in illustrating how cooperation and solidarity can be achieved. This is already taking place in areas such as informal learning, with examples of mutual aid among older people and intergenerational learning which brings together students drawn from different age groups. The former is illustrated by the University of the Third Age (U3A), first established in France in 1972 and developed in the UK since 1981. Here, members become teachers as well as learners, fostering a 'self-help' ideal based on the knowledge that retired people are experts in many fields. By 2010, U3A had established more than 200 groups in the UK with a membership reaching beyond 200,000. Another important area for informal education has been the development of 'intergenerational learning' – i.e., educational programmes which link older with younger learners. Newman and Hatton-Yeo (2008) cite the example of the NUGRAN programme at the University of Valencia, which creates learning experiences that cross the generations, involving older and younger adults together, with the aim of promoting greater contact, trust and more positive attitudes between them. The programme began with 71 students in 1999 and had expanded to 1,000 by 2007. Achenbaum (2005: 61) provides similar examples from the US, citing in particular the partnership between the University of North Carolina at Asheville and the North Carolina Center for Creative Retirement: 'Participants take classes that they design, conduct intergenerational programs to develop leadership skills, and analyze problems in the community and at the state level.'[3]

Another form of intergenerational solidarity recognizes the common interests of older and younger generations in protecting and improving the environment. Steinig and Butts (2010: 64) emphasize that:

> Older adults are concerned about the world they are leaving behind for their grandchildren and other younger generations. The young are concerned about the state of the world they will inherit. Both populations are often particularly susceptible to the same environmental health hazards – air pollution days for example. They are each at an age when they are more likely to live life in their neighbourhoods and have more flexibility in their schedules than working, commuting middle generations.

Pillemer et al. (2010) argue that older people represent an important source for creating solutions to environmental problems through volunteering and civic engagement, drawing upon their own knowledge and experience (see also Achenbaum, 2005). Steinig and Butts (2010), discussing the US experience, highlight the fact that intergenerational strategies can have a positive impact on the environment through shared sites and housing developments that bring generations together. More generally, such work has the benefit of bringing together 'the collective resources of the aging and environmental constituencies to encourage senior volunteers to work together to enhance a community's environment for present and future generations' (Wright and Lund, 2010: 15).

Generational and friendship solidarities

Social ties linked with family and friends represent another significant area for the development of new forms of solidarity. Older people have always been viewed within the context of family ties, with the idea – developed in the work of Ethel Shanas (1979) – that older people turn first to their immediate family for care and support. Research in social science provides contrasting views on the influences affecting family life. Evidence from different countries (reviewed in Chapter 6) demonstrates that intergenerational ties continue to be important across the life course.[4] Against this, the growth of individualism, as identified by sociologists such as Beck and Giddens, suggests a loosening of kinship bonds but with other non-kin ties moving to occupy a more prominent position. On the first point, the significance of intergenerational solidarities in the lives of older people remains substantial. Research in France by Arber and Attias-Donfut (2000) highlights the role of the middle, or 'pivot', generation in providing economic support to young people on the threshold of adulthood, as well as in providing flexible forms of care for parents in late age. They summarize the range of solidarities in the following way:

> Within the life course, individuals begin by receiving support from their mid-life parents which they in turn indirectly repay in their economically active years through the provision of pensions. During this period they also provide to their adult children and receive private transfers from their elderly parents who in turn benefit from care as they enter later life. (2000: 65)

Bengtson et al. (2003) make the point that multigenerational family bonds are becoming increasingly significant in family life, given the more complex partnerships characteristic of society. The demographic changes discussed in Chapter 2 – increased life expectancy and reductions in fertility – are producing what has been termed a 'beanpole' family structure, one with more generations alive but with fewer members in each generation. These trends provide opportunities for new forms of social solidarity. Prolonged periods of grandparenting (often lasting for three decades or more for grandmothers) are a novel experience compared with previous centuries. Thompson argues that grandparenting may be viewed as a distinctively modern experience – in the past, 'because they died earlier, two-thirds of children grew up without significant memory of a grandparent' (1999: 476). This may be contrasted with the findings of the French study by Arber and Attias-Donfut (2000), which revealed that, in their sample, two out of three of the middle generation provided care to grandchildren, whether on a regular basis or occasionally during the entire year and often during vacations. Such findings have been confirmed in European research (Arber and Timonen, 2012) and in the US (Minkler, 1999). Minkler demonstrated the dramatic rise in grandparenting care through the 1980s and 1990s, with more than 1 in 10 grandparents having primary responsibility for raising a grandchild at some point, with care often lasting for several years. The key role of grandparents has been confirmed in many countries in the global south, especially in relation to care provided to children orphaned by HIV/AIDS. More than 60 per cent of orphaned children live in grandparent-headed households in Nambia, South Africa and Zimbabwe, and more than 50 per cent in Botswana, Malawi and Tanzania. According to UN estimates, about 11 million children have been orphaned by HIV/AIDS in sub-Saharan Africa. Data from 27 countries in the region show that the extended family takes care of 9 out of 10 of these orphans, and in most cases responsibility for care falls upon grandparents, usually the grandmother (Knodel et al., 2002)

Such findings – in different cultural settings – underline the accuracy of Bengtson et al.'s (2000: 9) view that, increasingly, older people are the 'donors, not the net recipients' of generational support. Furthermore, Künemund and Rein (1999: 97) have made the important observation that providing public resources to older people may assist in raising levels of emotional support within the family. They conclude: 'When elderly people have sufficient resources of their own, they are not forced by necessity to rely upon their families. Therefore interactions focused on intimacy and closeness have the potential to develop.'

New solidarities will also emerge from greater diversity in the types of relationships experienced in later life. This will arise from trends associated with the growing importance of single person households and the growth in the numbers of people (across all age groups) living alone (Klinenberg, 2012) together with the spread of transnational ties associated with global migration (see Chapter 6). Instead of people being locked into family groups, they are more likely to be 'managing' a spread of relationships – or 'personal communities', to use Wellman and Wortley's (1990) phrase – with friends, kin, neighbours and other ties, giving and receiving help at different points over the life course. Among these ties, following the work of Pahl (2000), friends are likely to be of major importance, in some cases replacing family as sources of support in old age. Ties of choice may be especially important in maintaining physical and mental health (Allan, 2010). This is borne out in studies in the UK and elsewhere which confirm the importance of the confidant in the lives of older people, with friends being crucial to this role (Phillipson et al., 2000). Allan (2010) makes the point that the ability to develop new informal solidarities in later life depends in part on the skills and personality of those involved. Over their lifetime some individuals become adept at developing new friendships; others find this more difficult. Institutional supports may be necessary to support the development and maintenance of such ties, along with appropriate resources on the part of the individual. An important development, however, is likely to be older people themselves forging new relationships and social ties. This will be the case whether living alone, or in a partnership, or in a residential community of some kind.

Caring solidarities

In respect of developing new or reinforcing existing solidarities, the case might also be made for reconnecting to the original vision of a welfare state with responsibility for promoting the well-being of all its citizens. The tendency for capitalism to convert 'public services into commodities' (Navarro, 1976) has been vastly accelerated since the turn of the century, with increasing penetration of multinational corporations into the health and social care system. The evidence suggests that this process has had the greatest effect on the poorest elderly, with community services for low-income groups most vulnerable to underfunding and potential closure (Hermann, 2009). Deppe (2009) draws a wider argument about the importance of what he calls 'protected social spaces, which are orientated to the common welfare and which cannot be trusted to the blind power of the market'. He argues:

> We have to respect and sustain areas in which communication and co-operation is not commercialised, where services do not have the character of commodities. Such protected sectors extend from the way vulnerable groups are dealt with . . . to social goals such as solidarity and equity and vulnerable communication structures – especially those which are based on confidence like the . . . worker–patient relationship. Indeed, these protected social spaces form the basis for a humane social model. (2009: 36)

Developing such spaces will be especially important given the need to protect people with Alzheimer's and other forms of dementia, as well as those with major physical disabilities, from the dangers of abusive relationships both in the community and in institutional settings. The more positive question here is how to develop new forms of cooperation in the process of managing health conditions which affect people in later life – for example, those associated with changes linked to dementia. The conventional approach is to see the increase in the number of people diagnosed with illnesses such as Alzheimer's disease as an impending 'time bomb' set to wreak havoc on health and social care systems. People with dementia are themselves viewed (see Chapter 8) in largely medicalized and depersonalized terms; indeed, it is precisely the loss of personality which is often presented as the most distressing aspect of the condition. But another view is possible about the nature of dementia – namely, that it provides the basis for developing new forms of collaboration and cooperation. This point is illustrated by relational and biographical approaches to dementia, where the focus is on challenging the story of decline associated with the illness, bringing out people's 'potential for vitality, fulfilment, and even wisdom' (George and Whitehouse, 2010: 351), and involving people diagnosed with dementia as co-investigators in the task of living with cognitive change. These seem big tasks and the challenge of dementia is precisely that it involves a questioning of many of the relationships developed in working with people in periods of vulnerability and insecurity.

Given the above context, one option for strengthening existing and developing new solidarities might come from the adoption of the type of human rights perspective developed in the later writings of Peter Townsend (2007). He highlighted the importance of measures such as the European Convention on Human Rights and the Universal Declaration of Human Rights as offering a means of challenging the 'structured dependency' of older people. Use of such frameworks may become essential given the rise of care organizations operating across national borders, and the drive to deregulate and privatize hitherto public services. Townsend argued that problems relating to dependency persisted as a major issue affecting older people, with these problems set to grow in many parts of the world. At the same time, he concluded:

> Human rights instruments offer hope of breaking down blanket discrimination and of using resources more appropriately, and more generously, according to severity of need. But investment in human rights is not only a moral and quasi-legal salvation from things that are going depressingly wrong. Used best, human rights offer a framework of thought and planning [for] the 21st Century that enables society to take a fresh, and more hopeful, direction. (2007: 43)

Global solidarities

Finally, the global challenge of population ageing requires more coherent analysis and policy development than is presently the case. Three points might be made in support of this: first, formulating policies that can have an impact on key transnational bodies is set to be a major task over the next few years. Groups representing older people must become connected with the larger organizations and forums (linked with the EC and UN) that are attempting to formulate a global agenda on social issues. Evidence for political activity among pensioners in a number of countries offers an important platform upon which to build an age-integrated movement for social change. The joining of movements of opposition to the worst abuses of globalization – currently largely youth-orientated (Mason, 2012) – is essential, and the role of older people's organizations is pivotal given moves to privatize public health and retirement programmes.

Second, the needs of older people in crisis and emergency situations require urgent attention. The onset of global warming, the acceleration of military conflict and the recurrence of famine and disease in low-income countries place older people at particular risk. They are especially vulnerable in periods of social and economic crisis, as they risk being displaced from their homes, separated from relatives, and facing disruption to supplies of food and healthcare. Notwithstanding this, HelpAge International (2004) argues:

> [D]onor agencies do not currently consider older people to be a high-risk group, to be targeted for food aid, in emergency situations . . . A greater awareness relating to the health and nutrition needs of older people in emergency areas is required among community-based organizations and local and international NGOs involved in relief programmes.

This point also applies equally to high- and low-income countries, as demonstrated in crises such as Hurricane Katrina (Bytheway, 2006), the 2003 heat wave in France (Ogg, 2005) and the 2011 earthquake and tsunami in Japan (Miramatsu and Akiyama, 2011). In all three cases, elderly people were disproportionately affected compared with other age groups, but failed to receive the specialist help and support required.

Third, the international community must take a stronger stand in monitoring policies directed at older people. Ageing units in IGOs are often understaffed or non-existent. The small United Nations Aging Group in New York, for instance, could be strengthened to play a major role in coordinating and consulting with IGOs and NGOs in initiatives affecting older people. Along those lines, NGOs and IGOs should collaborate to implement a programme designed to develop and disseminate best practices following the example of the WHO 'International Mental Health Collaborating Network'. At the same time, the power of IGOs such as the IMF and World Bank to impose social policies resulting in reductions in expenditure on services and pensions presently goes unchallenged. This has been a particular feature of economic programmes directed at Latin American and East European countries and is in conflict with aspirations to build a secure and dignified old age across the global community.

Conclusion

The argument of this chapter, reflecting the book more generally, has been that the benefits of population ageing should be viewed in terms of the development of new forms of solidarity across different age and social groups. Older people have been especially vulnerable to the charge of contributing to economic crisis and divisions between generations. At the same time, the stakes are high regarding the future of policies influencing the lives of older people. As John Gray (2010: 5) has observed: 'A roll-back of the state of the magnitude [planned] will leave people more exposed to the turbulence of world markets than they have been for generations. Inevitably, they will seek protection.' Yet the nature of such support will be different from that which shaped the lives of older people in the second half of the twentieth century. Then, it was a relatively modest welfare state which provided a 'moral narrative' for growing old; then, it was the promise of retirement which underpinned the aspirations of many, at least in industrial countries; then, it was the idea of a contract between generations which was presented as a new form of 'bonding' for society. Analysis now suggests a more unequal and divided old age, with prosperity for some matched by deep poverty for others, all of this complicated by the greater spread of incomes within different cohorts and added threats introduced by global risks and insecurities.

But at the very least all this should be seen as a challenge to develop new forms of analysis and policy alternatives. Social research is now faced with examining a different type of ageing, underpinned by changing institutional forces and responses. These are transforming the landscape around which the social construction of ageing has traditionally been built. Social research has been slow to respond to the changes facing older people, notably those most affected by policies which undermine traditional sources of support. Developing fresh ways of analysing and responding to the challenge of population ageing is likely to remain at centre stage in analytical and policy debate for some years ahead. This book provides a small contribution to this important process.

Notes

1 **Introduction: Understanding Ageing**

1 The literature on and by the boomer generation expanded at a rapid rate through the 2000s. Some examples include: Diski (2009) with a biographical account; Buckley (2007) and Grant (2010) with fictional accounts; Willetts (2010) a critical review of potential tensions between generations; Phillipson et al. (2008) an overview of the construction of boomers as a 'problem' generation; Bonvalet and Ogg (2011) on the housing and consumption experiences of boomers.

2 These reports will be discussed in Chapter 8 of this book.

3 Athill (2008) provides a powerful account of her own ageing; Davidson (1997) the challenge of caring for someone with dementia.

2 **Ageing Societies in a Global Perspective**

1 For a discussion of fears about population decline during the 1920s and 1930s, see Thane (2000): ch. 7.

2 Median age: the age at which half the population is younger and half the population is older.

3 For further discussion on issues relating to demographic change in China, see Powell and Cook (2007).

4 These figures are taken from the 2008 English Longitudinal Study of Ageing, Wave 4 (Banks et al., 2010).

5 See Calasanti (2010) for a comprehensive review of issues relating to gender inequality and globalization.

3 Social Theories of Ageing

1 For a review of humanistic perspectives on ageing, see Cole et al., 1992; 2010.

6 Ageing and Pensions: The Social Construction of Inequality

1 A number of terms relating to pensions are used in this chapter, definitions for the key ones are as follows:
- Private pension income: refers to income from all non-state pensions, including (unless otherwise stated) public sector occupational pension schemes.
- State benefit income: refers to retirement pension (the Basic State Pension and additional state pensions) plus income from related benefits such as pension credit, disability living allowance, attendance allowance, incapacity allowance and winter fuel allowance.
- Defined Benefit Scheme (DB): a pension scheme in which the rules specify the rate of benefits to be paid. The most common DB scheme is a salary-related scheme in which the benefits are based on the number of years of pensionable service.
- Defined Contribution Scheme (DC): a pension scheme in which the benefits are determined by the contributions paid into the scheme, the investment returned on those contributions, and the type of annuity purchased upon retirement. DC pensions are sometimes referred to as 'money purchase schemes'.
- Scheme status: an occupational pension scheme may be open, closed, frozen or winding up. An open scheme admits new members; a closed scheme does not admit new members but may continue to accrue pension rights; in a frozen scheme, benefits continue to be payable to existing members but no new members are admitted, and no further benefits accrue to existing members.
2 Harrison (2012) illustrates this point with a number of case studies.

10 Conclusion: New Pathways for Later Life

1 For a comprehensive overview of the work of Peter Townsend, see Walker et al., 2010.
2 See, e.g., Age Concern, *Millennium Papers: The Debate of the Age* (1999).
3 See Phillipson and Ogg (2010) for a more extensive review of university-based education programmes.
4 For a review of intergenerational relationships and support in a global context, see International Longevity Centre Global Alliance Report (2012)

References

Abel-Smith, B. & Townsend, P. (1965) *The Poor and the Poorest*. Bell, London.

Aboderin, I. (2010) Global Ageing: Perspectives from Sub-Saharan Africa. In Dannefer, D. & Phillipson, C. (eds), *The Sage Handbook of Social Gerontology*. Sage Books, London, pp. 405–429.

Achenbaum, W.A. (2005) *Older Americans, Vital Communities*. John Hopkins University Press, Baltimore.

Achenbaum, W.A. (2010) Past as Prologue: Toward a Global History of Ageing. In Dannefer, D. & Phillipson, C. (eds), *The Sage Handbook of Social Gerontology*. Sage Books, London, pp. 20–32.

Age Concern (1999) *Millennium Papers: The Debate of the Age*. Age Concern, Mitchum.

Age UK (2011) *Care in Crisis: Causes and Solutions*. Age UK, London.

Aldridge, F. & Tuckett, A. (2007) *What Older People Learn*. National Institute of Adult and Continuing Education, Leicester.

Allan, G. (2010) Friendship and Ageing. In Dannefer, D. & Phillipson, C. (eds), *The Sage Handbook of Social Gerontology*. Sage Books, London, pp. 239–248.

Allan, G. & Crow, G. (2001) *Families, Households and Society*. Palgrave, London.

Alzheimer's Society (2009) *Counting the Cost: Caring for People with Dementia on Hospital Wards*. Alzheimer's Society, London.

American Council on Education (2007) *Older Adults and Higher Education*. ACE, London.

Arber, S. & Attias-Donfut, C. (eds) (2000) *The Myth of Generational Conflict: The Family and State in Ageing Societies*. Routledge, London.

Arber, S. & Timonen, V. (eds) (2012) *Contemporary Grandparenting: Changing Family Relationships in a Global Context*. Policy Press, Bristol.

Arnold, G. (2012) *Migration: Changing the World*. Pluto Press, London.

Association of Consulting Actuaries (2012) *Workplace Pensions: Challenging Times*. ACA, London.

Atchley, A. (2000) *Continuity and Adaptation in Aging*. John Hopkins University Press, Baltimore.

Atchley, R. (1971) Retirement and Leisure Participation. *The Gerontologist* 11, 13–17.

Athill, D. (2008) *Somewhere Towards the End*. Granta, London.

Baars, J. (2009) Problematic Foundations: Theorizing Time, Age and Aging. In Bengtson, V., Gans, D., Putney, N. & Silverstein, M. (eds), *Handbook of Theories of Aging*, 2nd edn. Springer, New York, pp. 87–100.

Baars, J. (2012) *Aging and the Art of Living*. John Hopkins University Press, Baltimore.

Baars, J., Dannefer, D., Phillipson, C. & Walker, A. (eds) (2006) *Aging, Globalization and Inequality*. Baywood Publishing Company, Amityville, NY.

Baldassar, L. (2007) Transnational Families and Aged Care: The Mobility of Care and Migrancy of Ageing. *Journal of Ethnic and Migration Studies* 33, 275–297.

Baldassar, L., Baldock, C.V. & Wilding, R. (2007) *Families Caring Across Borders*, Palgrave, London.

Baltes, P. & Baltes, M. (1990) *Successful Aging: Perspectives from the Behavioural Sciences*. Cambridge University Press, Cambridge.

Banks, J. et al. (eds) (2010) *Financial Circumstances, Health and Well-being of the Older Population in England. The 2008 English Longitudinal Study of Ageing*. Institute of Fiscal Studies, London.

Bartlam, B., Lally, F. & Crome, P. (2010) Drug Trials and Older People: Time to Embrace the Complexity of Age. *Drugs and Ageing* 28, 679–680.

Basch, L., Schiller, N. & Szanton Blanc, C. (1994) *Nations Unbound: Transnational Projects, Postcolonial Predicaments and Deterritorialized Nation-States*. Gordon & Breach, Langhorne, PA.

Basting, A. (2001) God is a Talking Horse: Dementia and the Performance of the Self. *The Drama Review* 45, 78–94.

Bauer, E. & Thompson, P. (2006) *Jamaican Hands Across the Atlantic*. Ian Randle Publishers, Kingston, Jamaica.

Bauman, Z. (1992) *Intimations of Postmodernity*. Blackwell, Oxford.

Bauman, Z. (1998) *Globalization: The Human Consequences*. Polity, Cambridge.

Bauman, Z. (2000) *Liquid Modernity*. Polity, Cambridge.

Beck, U. (1992) *Risk Society*. Sage Books, London.

Beck, U. (2000) Living Your Own Life in a Runaway World: Individualisation, Globalisation and Politics. In Hutton, W. & Giddens, A. (eds), *On The Edge: Living with Global Capitalism*. Jonathan Cape, London, pp. 164–174.

Becker, H. (1963) *Outsiders: Studies in the Sociology of Deviance*. Free Press, New York.

Bengtson, V.L. (1993) Is the 'Contract Across Generations' Changing? Effects of Population Aging on Obligations and Expectations Across Age Groups. In Bengtson, V.L. & Achenbaum, W.A. (eds), *The Changing Contract Across Generations*. Aldine de Gruyter, New York, pp. 3–24.

Bengtson, V.L. & Putney, N. (2006) Future 'Conflicts' Across Generations and Cohorts? in Vincent, J., Phillipson, C. & Downs, M. (eds), *The Futures of Old Age*. Sage Books, London, pp. 20–29.

Bengtson, V.L., Gans, D., Putney, N. & Silverstein, M. (eds) (2009) *Handbook of Theories of Aging*, 2nd edn. Springer, New York.

Bengston, V.L., Giarrusso, R., Silverstein, M. & Wang, H. (2000) Families and Intergenerational Families in Ageing Societies. *Hallym International Journal of Aging* 2, 3–10.

Bengtson, V.L., Lowenstein, A., Putney, N. & Gans, D. (2003) Global Aging and the Challenge to Families. In Bengtson, V.L. & Lowenstein, A. (eds), *Global Aging and Challenges to Families*. Aldine de Gruyter, New York, pp. 1–26.

Berger, P. & Luckmann, T. (1967) *The Social Construction of Reality*. Penguin, London.

Berry, C. (2012) *The Rise of Gerontocracy: Addressing the Intergenerational Deficit*. Intergenerational Foundation, London.

Best, F. (1980) *Flexible Life Scheduling*. Praeger, New York.

Beveridge, W. (1942) *Social Insurance and Allied Services*. HMSO, London.

Binstock, R. & Fishman, J. (2010) Social Dimensions of Anti-Ageing Medicine and Science. In Dannefer, D. & Phillipson, C. (eds), *The Sage Handbook of Social Gerontology*. Sage Books, London, pp. 472–482.

Binstock, R. & George, L. (eds) (2011) *Handbook of Aging and the Social Sciences*, 7th edn. Academic Press, San Diego, CA.

Blackburn, R. (2002) *Banking on Death*. Verso, London.

Blackburn, R. (2006) *Age Shock: How Finance Is Failing Us*. Verso, London.

Blaikie, A. (2006) *Ageing and Popular Culture*. Cambridge University Press, Cambridge.

Blau, Z. (1973) *Old Age in a Changing Society*. New Viewpoints, New York.

Blossfield, H.-P., Mills, M. & Bernardi, F. (eds) (2006) *Globalization, Uncertainty and Men's Careers*. Routledge, London.

Bonvalet, C. and Ogg, J (2011) *Baby Boomers: A Mobile Generation*. Bardwell Press, Oxford.

Botelho, L. (2005) The 17th Century. In Thane, P. (ed.), *The Long History of Old Age*. Thames and Hudson, London, pp. 113–174.

Bourdieu, P. (1977) *Outline of a Theory of Practice*. Cambridge University Press, Cambridge.

Bourdieu, P. (1986) Forms of Capital. In Richardson, J. (ed.), *Handbook of Theory and Research for the Sociology of Education*. Greenwood, New York, pp. 378–98.

Brewin Dolphin (2008) *Pensions at Risk from Debt Repayments*. At http://www.brewindolphinmedia.co.uk/media/press-releases-and-comment/2008/march/2008–03–24.aspx. Accessed 12 September 2012.

Brimstone, B. (2011) Labelling Matters: Households Spend 40% of Winter Fuel Payment on Fuel. *Press Release,* Institute for Fiscal Studies, 8 June.

Browne, J. (2011) *Living Standards During the Recession*. Institute for Fiscal Studies, London.

Buckley, C (2007) *Boomsday: A Novel*. Allison and Busby, London.

Buffel, T. & Phillipson, C. (2012) Experiences of Place among Older Migrants Living in Inner-City Neighbourhoods in Belgium and England. *Diversité urbaine* 11, 13–38.

Burgess, E.W. (1960) Aging in Western Culture. In Burgess, E.W. (ed.), *Aging in Western Societies*. University of Chicago Press, Chicago, pp. 3–28.

Burns, B. & Phillipson, C (1986) *Drugs, Aging and Society: Social and Pharmacological Perspectives*. Croom Helm, London.

Burrow, J. (1986) *The Ages of Man*. Oxford University Press, Oxford.

Burtless, G. (2009) Financial Market Turbulence and Social Security Reform. In Orenstein, M. (ed.), *Pensions, Social Security, and the Privatization of Risk*. Social Science Research Council Series on the Privatization of Risk. Columbia University Press, New York, pp. 72–85.

Bury, M. (1991) The Sociology of Chronic Illness: A Review of Research and Prospects. *Sociology of Health and Illness* 13, 451–468.

Butler, R. (1975) *Why Survive? Being Old in America.* Harper & Row, New York.

Bytheway, W. (2009) Writing About Age: Birthdays and the Passage of Time. *Ageing and Society* 29, 883–901.

Bytheway, W. (2006) The Evacuation of Older People: The Case of Hurricane Katrina. Paper presented at the annual conference of the Royal Geographical Society and Institute of British Geographers, London, 31 August 2006.

Calasanti, T. (2010) Gender and Ageing in the Context of Globalization. In Dannefer, D. & Phillipson, C. (eds), *The Sage Handbook of Social Gerontology.* Sage Books, London, pp. 137–149.

Callahan, D. (1987) *Setting Limits: Medical Goals in an Aging Society.* Touchstone Books, New York.

Callender, C. & Heller, D. (2009) The Future of Student Funding. In Withers, K. (ed.), *First Class? Challenges and Opportunities for the UK's University Sector.* Institute for Public Policy Research, London, pp. 56–72.

Care Quality Commission (2009) *The State of Health Care and Adult Social Care in England.* The Stationery Office, London.

Care Quality Commission (2011a) *Dignity and Nutrition: Inspection Programme.* CQC, London.

Care Quality Commission (2012) *Failing the Frail: A Chaotic Approach to Commissioning Healthcare Services for Care Homes.* CQC, London.

Chambers, P., Allan, G., Phillipson, C. & Ray, M. (2009) *Family Practices in Later Life.* Policy Press, Bristol.

Chatzitheochari, S. & Arber, S. (2011) Identifying the Third Agers: An Analysis of British Retirees' Leisure Pursuits. *Sociological Research Online* 16. At http://www.socresonline.org.uk/16/4/3.html. Accessed 12 September 2012.

Cheung, S. & McKay, S. (2010) *Training and Progression in the Labour Market. Research Report 680.* Department for Work and Pensions, London.

Christensen, K., Doblhammer, G., Rau, R. & Vaupel, J. (2009) Ageing Populations: The Challenges Ahead. *The Lancet* 374, 1196–1208.

Chudacoff, H. (1989) *How Old Are You? Age Consciousness in American Culture.* Princeton University Press, Princeton.

Clery, E., McKay, S., Phillips, M., & Robinson, C. (2007) *Attitudes to Pensions: The 2006 Survey (Research Report 434).* Department for Work and Pensions, London.

Coates, K. & Silburn, R. (1970) *Poverty: The Forgotten Englishmen*. Penguin, London.

Cole, T. (1992) *The Journey of Life*. Cambridge University Press, Cambridge.

Cole, T., Ray, M. & Kastenbaum, R. (2010) *A Guide to Humanistic Studies in Ageing: What Does It Mean to Grow Old?* John Hopkins University Press, Baltimore.

Cole, T., Tassel, D. & Kastenbaum, R. (eds) (1992) *Handbook of the Humanities and Aging*. Springer, New York.

Coleman, J.S. (1990) *Foundations of Social Theory*. Harvard University Press, Cambridge, MA.

Commission on Dignity in Care for Older People (2012) *Delivering Dignity: Securing Dignity in Care for Older People in Hospitals and Care Homes. A Report for Consultation.* Local Government Association/NHS Confederation/Age UK, London.

Cory, C. (2012) *Unfinished Business: Barriers and Opportunities for Older Workers*. The Resolution Foundation, London.

Cowgill, D.O. & Holmes, L.D. (eds) (1972) *Aging and Modernization*. Appleton-Century-Crofts, New York.

Cowling, C. (2010) *Pension Reckoning: Paying for Private and Public Pensions*. Politeia, London.

Crawford, M. (1971) Retirement and Disengagement. *Human Relations* 24, 217–236.

Cribier, F. (1981) Changing Retirement Patterns: The Experience of a Cohort of Parisian Salaried Workers. *Ageing and Society* 1, 51–71.

Crystal, S. (2006) Dynamics of Late-Life Inequality: Modelling the Interplay of Health Disparities, Economic Resources and Public Policies. In Baars, J., Dannefer, D., Phillipson, C. & Walker, A. (eds), *Aging, Globalization and Inequality: The New Critical Gerontology*. Baywood Publishing Company, Amityville, NY, pp. 183–204.

Crystal, S. & Shea, D. (2003) Cumulative Advantage, Cumulative Disadvantage, and Inequality Among Older People. *The Gerontologist* 30, 437–443.

Cumming, E. & Henry, W.E. (1961) *Growing Old: The Process of Disengagement*. Basic Books, New York.

Czaja, S. & Sharit, J. (2009) *Aging and Work: Issues and Implications in a Changing Landscape*. John Hopkins University Press, Baltimore.

Daatland, S.-O. (2003) Time to Pay Back? Is There Something for Psychology and Sociology in Gerontology? In Andersson, L. (ed.), *Cultural Gerontology*, Auburn House, Westport, CT, pp. 1–13.

Dannefer, D. (1999) Neoteny, Naturalization and Other Constituents of Human Development. In Ryff, C. & Marshall, B. (eds), *Self and Society: Aging Processes*. Springer, New York, pp. 67–93.

Dannefer, D. (2000) Bringing Risk Back In: The Regulation of the Self. In Schaie, K.W. & Hendricks, J. (eds), *The Evolution of the Aging Self*. Springer Publishing, New York, pp. 269–280.

Dannefer, D. (2003) Cumulative Advantage/Disadvantage and the Life Course: Cross Fertilizing Age and Social Science Theory. *Journal of Gerontology* 58B, 327–337.

Dannefer, D. (2011) Age, the Life Course and the Sociological Imagination: Prospects for Theory. In Binstock, R. & George, L. (eds), *Handbook of Aging and the Social Sciences*, 7th edn. Academic Press, San Diego, CA, pp. 3–16.

Dannefer, D. & Kelly–Moore, J. (2009) Theorizing the Life Course: New Twists in the Paths. In Bengtson, V., Gans, D., Putney, N. & Silverstein, M. (eds), *Handbook of Theories of Aging*, 2nd edn. Springer, New York, pp. 389–412.

Dannefer, D. & Phillipson, C. (eds) (2010) *The Sage Handbook of Social Gerontology*. Sage Books, London.

Dannefer, D. & Settersten, R. (2010) The Study of the Life Course: Implications for Social Gerontology. In Dannefer, D. & Phillipson, C. (eds), *The Sage Handbook of Social Gerontology*. Sage Books, London, pp. 3–19.

Davidson, A. (1997) *Alzheimer's: A Love Story*. Carol Publishing Company, Seacaucus, NJ.

Deacon, A. (2000) Globalization and Social Policy: The Threat to Equitable Welfare. At http://www.unrisd.org/ 80256B3C005BCCF9/(httpPublications)/815BC5D09E74323A 80256B67005B740A?OpenDocument. Accessed 12 September 2012.

Dench, S. & Regan, J. (2000) *Learning in Later Life: Motivation and Impact*. Research Report RR183. Department for Education and Employment, London.

Department for Education and Skills (DfES) (2005) *Skills: Getting on in Business, Getting on at Work*. Parts 1–3. The Stationery Office, London.

Department of Energy and Climate Change (2012) *Annual Report on Fuel Poverty Statistics 2012*. DECC, London.

Department of Social Security (1997) *Welfare Reform Focus File*. Central Office of Information, London.

Department for Work and Pensions (2008) *The Pensioners' Income Series*. DWP, London.

Department for Work and Pensions (2009) *Building a Society for All Ages*. DWP, London.

Department for Work and Pensions (2011a) *Number of Future Centenarians by Age Group.* DWP, London.

Department for Work and Pensions (2011b) *Family Resources Survey 2009/10.* DWP, London.

Department for Work and Pensions (2012) *The Pensioners' Income Series 2010–2011.* DWP, London.

Dex, S. & Phillipson, C. (1986) Social Policy and the Older Worker. In Phillipson, C. & Walker, A. (eds), *Ageing and Social Policy: A Critical Assessment.* Gower Books, Aldershot.

Deppe, H.-U. (2009) The Nature of Health Care: Commodification Versus Solidarity. In Panitch, L. & Leys, C. (eds), *Morbid Symptoms: Health under Capitalism* (Socialist Register 2010). Merlin Press, London, pp. 29–38.

Diamond, P. (2010) *How Globalisation is Changing Patterns of Marginalisation and Inclusion.* Joseph Rowntree Foundation, York.

Dilnot Commission (2011) *Commission on Funding of Care and Support.* At www.dilnotcommission.dh.gov.uk/. Accessed 12 September 2012.

Diski, J. (2009) *The Sixties.* Profile Books, London.

Dixon, S. (2003) Implications of Population Ageing for the Labour Market. *Labour Market Trends* 111, 67–76.

Donahue, W., Orbach, H. & Pollak, O. (1960) Retirement: The Emerging Social Pattern. In Tibbitts, C. (ed.), *Handbook of Social Gerontology: Societal Aspect of Aging.* University of Chicago Press, Chicago, pp. 330–406.

Dorling, D. (2011) *Injustice: Why Social Inequality Persists.* Policy Press, Bristol.

Douthit, K. (2006) Dementia in the Iron Cage: The Biopsychiatric Construction of Alzheimer's Dementia. In Baars, J., Dannefer, D., Phillipson, C. & Walker, A. (eds), *Aging, Globalization and Inequality.* Baywood Publishing Company, Amityville, NY, pp.159–182.

Dowd, J.J. (1975) Aging as Exchange: A Preface to Theory. *Journal of Gerontology* 30, 584–594.

Downs, M. & Bowers, B. (eds) (2008) *Excellence in Dementia Care: Research Into Practice.* Open University Press, Maidenhead.

Durkheim, E. (1933) *The Division of Labour in Society.* Free Press, New York.

Ekerdt, D. (2010) Frontiers of Research on Work and Retirement. *Journal of Gerontology: Social Sciences* 65B, 69–80.

Elder, G.H. (1974) *Children of the Great Depression.* University of Chicago Press, Chicago.

Elliott, A. & Lemert, C. (2006) *The New Individualism: The Emotional Costs of Globalization.* Routledge, London.

Estes, C.L. (2006) Critical Feminist Perspectives, Aging and Social Policy. In Baars, J., Dannefer, D., Phillipson, C. & Walker, A. (eds), *Aging, Globalization and Inequality: The New Critical Gerontology*. Baywood Publishing Company, Amityville, NY, pp.59–80.

Estes, C.L. (1979) *The Aging Enterprise*. Jossey-Bass, San Francisco.

Estes, C.L. (1981) The Social Construction of Reality: A Framework for Inquiry. In Lee, P.R., Ramsay, N.B. & Red, I. (eds), *The Nation's Health*. Boyd and Fraser, San Francisco, pp. 395–402.

Estes, C.L. (1999) Critical Gerontology and the New Political Economy of Aging. In Minkler, M. & Estes, C.L. (eds), *Critical Gerontology*. Baywood Publishing Company, Amityville, NY, pp. 17–36.

Estes, C.L. & Associates (2001) *Social Policy: A Critical Perspective*. Sage Books, New York.

Estes, C.L. & Binney, E.A. (1989) The Biomedicalization of Aging: Dangers and Dilemmas. *The Gerontologist* 29, 587–596.

Estes, C.L. & Phillipson, C. (2003) The Globalization of Capital, the Welfare State and Old Age Policy. *International Journal of Health Services* 32, 279–297.

Estes, C.L., Biggs, S. & Phillipson, C. (2003) *Social Theory, Social Policy and Ageing: A Critical Introduction*. Open University Press, Maidenhead.

European Commission (1999) *Active Ageing: Pivot of Policies for Older People in the New Millennium*. EC, Brussels.

European Commission (2009) *Intergenerational Solidarity: Summary*. EC, Brussels.

Featherstone, M., & Wernick, A. (eds) (1995) *Images of Ageing: Cultural Representations of Later Life*. Routledge, London.

Feinstein, L., Anderson, T., Hammond, C., Jamieson, A. & Woodley, A. (2007) *The Social and Economic Benefits of Part-Time, Mature Study at Birkbeck College and the Open University*. Open University/Birkbeck College, Milton Keynes/London.

Felstead, A. (2010) Closing the Age Gap? Age, Skills and the Experience of Work in Great Britain, *Ageing & Society* 30, 1293–1314.

Ferge, Z. (1997a) A Central European Perspective on the Social Quality of Europe. In Beck, W., van der Maesen, L. & Walker, A. (eds), *The Social Quality of Europe*. Kluwyer International, The Hague, pp.89–108.

Ferge, Z. (1997b) The Changed Welfare Paradigm: The Individualization of the Social, *Social Policy & Social Administration*, 31, 20–44.

Finch, J. & Mason, J. (1993) *Negotiating Family Responsibilities.* Routledge, London.

Fischer, D.H. (1977) *Growing Old in America.* Oxford University Press, Oxford.

Fokkema, T., Bekke, S. & Dykstra, P. (2008) *Solidarity Between Parents and their Adult Children in Europe.* Netherlands Interdisciplinary Demographic Institute. KNAW Press, Amsterdam.

Foner, A. (2000) Age Integration or Age Conflict as Society Ages? *The Gerontologist* 40, 272–6.

Foot, C. & Harrison, T. (2011) *How to Improve Cancer Survival: Explaining England's Relatively Poor Rates.* King's Fund & Cancer Research UK, London.

Ford, G. (2005) *Am I Still Needed? Guidance and Learning for Older Adults.* The Centre for Guidance Studies, University of Derby.

Formosa, M. (2009) *Class Dynamics in Later Life.* LIT Verlag, Zurich.

Frankenberg, R. (1966) *Communities in Britain.* Penguin Books, London.

Gardner, K. (1995) *Global Migrants, Local Lives.* Oxford University Press, Oxford.

Gardner, K. (2002) *Age, Narrative and Migration.* Berg, Oxford.

George, D. & Whitehouse, P. (2010) Dementia and Mild Cognitive Impairment in Social and Cultural Context. In Dannefer, D. & Phillipson, C. (eds), *The Sage Handbook of Social Gerontology.* Sage Books, London, pp. 343–356.

George, V. & Wilding, P. (2002) *Globalization and Human Welfare.* Palgrave, London.

Giddens, A. (1991) *Modernity and Self-identity.* Polity, Cambridge.

Giddens, A. (1994) *The Constitution of Society: Outline of the Theory of Structuration.* Polity, Cambridge.

Gilleard, C. & Higgs, P (2010) Aging Without Agency: Theorizing the Fourth Age. *Aging and Mental Health* 14, 121–128.

Gilleard, C. & Higgs, P. (2000) *Cultures of Ageing: Self, Citizen and the Body.* Prentice Hall, London.

Gilleard, C. & Higgs, P. (2005) *Contexts of Ageing: Class, Culture and Community.* Polity, Cambridge.

Gilleard, C. & Higgs, P. (2011) Consumption and Aging. In Settersten, R., Jr. & Angel, J. (eds), *Handbook of Sociology of Aging.* Springer Publishing, New York, pp. 361–378.

Gillion, C., Turner, J., Bailey, C. & Latulippe, D. (2000) *Social Security Pensions: Development and Reform.* International Labour Organisation, Geneva.

Ginn, J. (2012) Auto-Enrolment into a DC World: How Will NEST Work for Women and the Low Paid? Paper to University of Westminster Pensions Research Network. 2 March, London.

Glyn, A. (2007) *Capitalism Unleashed*. Oxford University Press, Oxford.

Goulborne, H. (1999) The Transnational Character of Caribbean Kinship in Britain. In S. McRae (ed.), *Changing Britain: Families and Households in the 1990s*. Oxford University Press, Oxford, pp. 176–199.

Gouldner, A. (1960) The Norm of Reciprocity: A Preliminary Statement. *American Sociological Review* 25, 161–178.

Gouldner, A. (1971) *The Coming Crisis of Western Sociology*. Heinemann Books, London.

Graebner, W. (1980) *A History of Retirement*. Yale University Press, New Haven.

Granovetter, M. (1973) The Strength of Weak Ties. *American Review of Sociology* 78, 1360–80.

Grant, L. (2010) *We Had It So Good*. Virago, London.

Gray, J. (2010) Progressive, Like the 1980s. *London Review of Books* 32, 3–7.

Greenhouse, S. (2008) *The Big Squeeze: Tough times for the American Worker*. Knopf, New York.

Grenier, A. (2012) *Transitions and the Lifecourse: Challenging the Constructions of 'Growing Old'*. Policy Press, Bristol.

Grundy, E., Murphy, M. & Shelton, N. (1999) Looking Beyond the Household: Intergenerational Perspectives on Living Kin and Contacts with Kin in Great Britain, *Population Trends* 97, 19–27.

Gubrium, J.F. (1986) *Oldtimers and Alzheimer's: The Descriptive Organization of Senility*. Jai Press, Greenwich, CT.

Guillemard, A.-M. (1989) The Trend Towards Early Labour Force Withdrawal and the Reorganisation of the Life Course. In Johnson, P., Conrad, C. & Thomson, D. (eds), *Workers versus Pensioners: Intergenerational Justice in an Ageing World*. Manchester University Press, Manchester, pp. 164–180.

Hagestad, G. & Dannefer, D. (2001) Concepts and Theories of Aging: Beyond Microfication in Social Science Approaches. In Binstock, R. & George, L. (eds), *Handbook of Aging and the Social Sciences*, 5th edn. Academic Press, San Diego, CA, pp. 3–21.

Hagestad, G. & Uhlenberg, P. (2007) The Impact of Demographic Changes on Relations Between Age Groups and Generations: A Comparative Perspective. In K.W. Schaie & P. Uhlenberg (eds), *Social Structures: Demographic Change and the Well-Being of Older Adults*. Springer Books, New York, pp. 239–261.

Hannah, L. (1986) *Inventing Retirement*. Cambridge University Press, Cambridge.

Harper, S. & Thane, P. (1989) The Consolidation of Old Age as a Phase of Life, 1945–1965. In Jeffreys, M. (ed.), *Growing Old in the Twentieth Century*. Routledge, London, pp. 43–61.

Harrington, M. (1963) *The Other America*. Penguin, London.

Harrison, D. (2012) *Treating DC Scheme Members Fairly in Retirement*. National Association of Pension Funders and Pensions Institute Research Report, London.

Havighurst, R.J. (1954) Flexibility and the Social Roles of the Retired. *American Journal of Sociology* 59, 309–11.

Heclo, H. (1989) Generational Politics. In Smeeding, T. & Torrey, B. (eds), *The Vulnerable*. Urban Institute Press, Washington, DC, pp. 381–441.

HelpAge International African Regional Development Centre (2004) *Summary of Research Findings on the Nutritional Status and Risk Factors for Vulnerability of Older People in Africa*. HelpAge International, Westlands, Nairobi.

Help the Aged (1979) *The Time of Your Life: A Handbook for Retirement*. Help the Aged, London.

Hendricks, J. (2003) Structure and Identity – Mind the Gap: Towards a Personal Resource Model of Successful Aging. In Biggs, S., Lowenstein, A. & Hendricks, J. (eds), *The Need for Theory: Critical Approaches to Social Gerontology*. Baywood Publishing Company, Amityville, NY, pp. 63–90.

Hennessy, P. (1993) *Never Again: Britain 1945–1951*. Vintage, London.

Hermann, C. (2009) The Marketisation of Health Care in Europe. In Panitch, L. & Leys, C. (eds), *Morbid Symptoms: Health Under Capitalism. The Socialist Register 2010*. Merlin Press, London, pp.125–145.

Higgs, P. & Gilleard, C. (2010) Generational Conflict, Consumption and the Ageing Welfare State in the United Kingdom. *Ageing and Society* 30, 1439–1451.

Higo, M. & Williamson, J. (2011) Global Aging. In Settersten, R. & Angel, J. (eds), *Handbook of Sociology of Aging*. Springer, New York, pp. 117–130.

Hills, J. (1996) Does Britain Have a Welfare Generation? In Walker, A. (ed.), *The New Generational Contract*. UCL Press; London, pp. 56–80.

Hills, J., Brewer, M., Jenkins, S., Lister, R., Lupton, R., Machin, S., Mills, C., Modood, T., Rees, T. & Riddell, S. (2010) *An Anatomy of Economic Inequality in the UK: Summary*. Government Equalities Office/Centre for Analysis of Social Exclusion, London.

Ho, C. (1991) *Salt-Water Trinnies: Afro-Trinidadian Immigrant Networks and Non-Assimilation in Los Angeles.* AMS Press, New York.

Hochschild, A. (1975) Disengagement Theory: A Critique and Proposal. *American Sociological Review* 40, 553–569.

Hockey, J. & James, A. (2003) *Social Identities Across the Life Course.* Palgrave Macmillan, London.

Hoff, A. & Tesch-Römer, C. (2007) Family Relations and Aging: Substantial Changes Since the Middle of the Last Century. In Wahl, H.-W., Tesch–Römer, C. & Hoff, A. (eds), *New Dynamics in Old Age: Individual, Environmental and Societal Perspectives.* Baywood Publishing Company, Amityville, NY, pp. 65–84.

Homer, P. and Holstein, M. (1990) *A Good Age?* Touchstone Books, New York.

House of Commons Health Committee (2012) *Social Care: Fourteenth Report of Session 2010–12.* The Stationery Office, London.

Howker, E. & Malik, S. (2010) *Jilted Generations: How Britain Has Bankrupted Its Youth.* Icon Books, London.

Hughes, M.E. & Waite, L. (2007) The Aging of the Second Demographic Transition. In Schaie, K.W. & Uhlenberg, P. (eds), *Social Structures: Demographic Change and the Well-being of Older Adults.* Springer Books, New York, pp. 179–212.

Humphrey, A., Costigan, P., Pickering, K., Stratford, N. & Barnes, M. (2003) *Factors Affecting the Labour Market: Participation of Older Workers.* Department for Work and Pensions, London.

International Longevity Centre Global Alliance Report (2012) *Global Perspectives on Multigenerational Households and Intergenerational Relations.* International Longevity Centre, London.

Jamieson, A. (2007) Higher Education Study in Later Life: What is the Point? *Ageing and Society* 27, 363–384.

Jenkins, A. (2011) Participation in Learning and Wellbeing Among Older Adults. *International Journal of Lifelong Education* 30(3), 403–420.

Jin, W., Joyce, R., Phillips, D. & Sibieta, L. (2011) *Poverty and Inequality in the UK: 2011.* Institute for Fiscal Studies, London.

John, R. (1984) Prerequistes of an Adequate Theory of Aging: A Critique and Reconceptualisation. *Mid-American Review of Sociology* 9, 79–108.

Johnson, P. & Falkingham, J. (1992) *Ageing and Economic Welfare.* Sage Books, London.

Johnson, P., Conrad, C. & Thomson, D. (eds) (1989) *Workers versus Pensioners: Intergenerational Justice in an Ageing World.* Manchester University Press, Manchester.

Jones, I.R., Hyde, M., Victor, C., Wiggins, R., Gilleard, C. & Higgs, P. (2008) *Ageing in a Consumer Society: From Passive to Active Consumption in Britain.* Policy Press, Bristol.

Judt, T. (2005) *Postwar: A History of Europe Since 1945.* Heinemann, London.

Judt, T. (2008) *Reappraisals: Reflections on the Forgotten Twentieth Century.* Penguin, London.

Judt, T. (2010) *Ill Fares the Land: A Treatise On Our Present Discontents.* Allen Lane, London.

Judt, T. (with Snyder, T.) (2012) *Thinking the Twentieth Century.* William Heinemann, London.

Kahn, R. & Antonucci, T. (1980) Convoys over the Life Course: Attachment, Roles and Social Support. In Baltes, P.B. & Brim, O. *Life-Span Development and Behaviour*, vol. 3. Academic Press, New York.

Kaplan, M. (1960) The Uses of Leisure. In Tibbitts, C. (ed.), *Handbook of Social Gerontology.* University of Chicago Press, Chicago, pp. 407–435.

Katz, S. (1996) *Disciplining Old Age: The Formation of Gerontological Knowledge.* University Press of Virginia, Charlottesville.

Katz, S. (2003) Critical Gerontological Theory: Intellectual Fieldwork and the Nomadic Life of Ideas. In Biggs, S., Lowenstein, A. & Hendricks, J. (eds), *The Need for Theory: Critical Approaches to Social Gerontology*, Baywood Publishing Company, Amityville, NY, pp.15–31.

Katz, S. (2010) Sociocultural Perspectives on Ageing Bodies. In Dannefer, D. & Phillipson, C. (eds), *The Sage Handbook of Social Gerontology.* Sage Books., London, pp. 357–366.

Kelly-Moore, J. & Lin, J. (2011) Widening the View: Capturing 'Unobserved' Heterogeneity in Studies of Age and the Life Course. In Settersten, R. & Angel, J. (eds), *Handbook of Sociology of Aging.* Springer, New York, pp. 51–70.

King, R. & Vullnetari, J. (2006) Orphan Pensioners and Migrating Grandparents: The Impact of Mass Migration on Older People. *Ageing and Society* 26: 783–816.

King's Fund (2009) *How Cold Will It Be? Prospects for NHS Funding 2011–2017.* King's Fund, London.

Kinsella, K. & He, W. (2009) *An Aging World 2008.* US Department of Health and Human Services, Washington, DC.

Kitwood, T. (1997) *Dementia Reconsidered: The Person Comes First.* Open University Press, Milton Keynes.

Klinenberg, E. (2012) *Going Solo: The Extraordinary Rise and Surprising Appeal of Living Alone.* Penguin, New York.

Knodel, J., Watkins, S. & Van Landingham, M. (2002) *AIDS and Older Persons: An International Perspective, PSC Research*

Report No. 02–495. Population Studies Center, University of Michigan.

Kohli, M. (1986) The World We Forgot: A Historical Review of the Life Course. In Marshall, V. (ed.), *Later Life*. Sage Books, London, pp. 271–303.

Kohli, M., Rein, M., Guillemard, A.-M. & Gunsteren, H.V. (eds) (1991) *Time for Retirement: Comparative Studies of Early Exit from the Labour Force*. Cambridge University Press, Cambridge.

Künemund, H. & M. Rein (1999) There Is More to Receiving than Needing: Theoretical Arguments and Empirical Explorations of Crowding In and Crowding Out. *Ageing and Society* 19, 93–121.

Kynaston, D. (2009) *Family Britain 1951–57*. Bloomsbury, London.

Lash, S. & Urry, J. (1987) *The End of Organized Capitalism*. Polity, Cambridge.

Laslett, P. (1989) *A Fresh Map of Life*. Weidenfeld & Nicolson, London.

Leach, R., Phillipson, C., Biggs, S. & Money, A. (2008) Sociological Perspectives on the Baby Boomers. *Quality in Ageing* 9, 19–26.

Liedtke, P. & Schanz, K.-U. (eds) (2012) *Addressing the Challenge of Global Ageing: Funding Issues and Insurance Solutions*. Geneva Association, Geneva.

Lievesley, N. (2010) *The Future Ageing of the Ethnic Minority Population of England and Wales*. Centre for Policy on Ageing, London.

Lissenburgh, S. & Smeaton, D. (2003) *Employment Transitions of Older Workers: The Role of Flexible Employment in Maintaining Labour Market Participation and Promoting Job Quality*. Policy Press, Bristol.

Litwak, E. (1960) Occupational Mobility and Extended Family Cohesion. *American Sociological Review* 25, 9–21.

Lloyd-Sherlock, P. (ed.) (2004) *Living Longer: Ageing, Development and Social Protection*. Zed Books, London.

Lloyd-Sherlock, P. (2010) *Population Ageing and International Development*. Policy Press, Bristol.

Longman, P. (1987) *Born to Pay*. Houghton Mifflin, Boston, MA.

Lowe, R. (1993) *The Welfare State in Britain since 1945*. Macmillan, London.

Lowenstein, A. (1999) Intergenerational Family Relations and Social Support. *Gerontologie und Geriatrie*. Key Note Lectures, Fifth European Congress of Gerontology. Steinkopff, Darmstadt, pp. 398–407.

Lowenstein, A. & Katz, R. (2010) Family and Age in a Global Context. In Dannefer, D. & Phillipson, C. (eds), *The Sage*

Handbook of Social Gerontology. Sage Books, London, pp. 190–201.

Lynott, R.J. & Lynott, P.P. (1996) Tracing the Course of Theoretical Development in the Sociology of Aging. *The Gerontologist* 36, 749–760.

McManners, J. (1985) *Death and the Enlightenment*. Oxford University Press, Oxford.

McNair, S. & Flynn, M. (2005) *The Age Dimension of Employment Practice: Employer Case Studies*. Department of Trade and Industry, London.

McNair, S., Flynn, M., Owen, L., Humphreys, C. & Woodfield, S. (2004) *Changing Work in Later Life: A Study of Job Transitions*, Centre for Research into the Older Workforce, University of Surrey.

Macnicol, J. (2006) *Age Discrimination: An Historical and Contemporary Analysis*. Cambridge University Press, Cambridge.

Mandelbaum, M. (2010) *The Frugal Superpower: America's Global Leadership in a Cash-Strapped Era*. Public Affairs, New York.

Mannheim, K. (1952) The Problem of Generations. *Essays on the Sociology of Knowledge*. Routledge & Kegan Paul, London.

Marmot, M., Allen, J., Goldblatt, P., Boyce, T., McNeish, D., Grady, M. & Geddes, I. (2010) *Fair Society, Healthy Lives: The Marmot Strategic Review of Health Inequalities in England Post-2010*. Department of Health, London.

Marshall, V. (1986) Dominant and Emerging Paradigms in the Social Psychology of Aging. In Marshall, V.W. (ed.), *Later Life: The Social Psychology of Aging*. Sage Books, California, pp. 9–31.

Marshall, V. & Clarke, P. (2010) Agency and Social Structure in Aging and Life-course Research. In Dannefer, D. & Phillipson, C. *The Sage Handbook of Social Gerontology*. Sage Books, London, pp. 294–305.

Mason, T. (2012) *Why It's All Kicking Off Everywhere: The New Global Revolutions*. Verso, London.

Matza, D. (1964) *Delinquency and Drift*. Wiley, New York.

Mayer, C. (2011) *Amortality: The Pleasures and Perils of Living Agelessly*. Vermillion, London.

Mayhew, K. & Rijkers, B. (2004) How to Improve the Human Capital of Older Workers, or the Sad Tale of the Magic Bullet. Paper prepared for the joint EC/OECD seminar, 'Human Capital and Labour Market Performance', Brussels.

Meyer, M.H. & Herd, P. (2007) *Market Friendly or Family Friendly? The State and Gender Inequality in Old Age*. Russell Sage Foundation, New York.

Minkler, M. (1999) Intergenerational Families Headed by Grand-parents: Contexts, Realities and Implications for Policy. *Journal of Aging Studies* 13, 199–218.

Minois, G. (1989) *History of Old Age*. Polity, Cambridge.

Miramatsu, N. & Akiyama, H. (2011) Japan: Super-Aging Society Preparing for the Future. *Gerontologist* 51, 425–432.

Moody, H. (1988) *Abundance of Life: Human Development Policies for an Aging Society*. Columbia University Press, New York.

Moody, H. (2010) *Aging: Concepts and Controversies*. Pine Forge Press, Los Angeles.

Morgan, D. (1996) *Family Connections: An Introduction to Family Studies*. Polity, Cambridge.

Mosley, L. & Uno, S. (2007) Racing to the Bottom or Climbing to the Top? Economic Globalization and Collective Labor Rights. *Comparative Political Studies* 40, 923–948.

Mullan, P. (2000) *The Imaginary Time Bomb: Why An Ageing Population Is Not a Social Problem*. I.B. Tauris, London.

Munnell. A. & Sass, S. (2008) *Working Longer: The Solution to the Retirement Income Challenge*. Brookings Institution Press, New York.

Mutchler, J. & Burr, J. (2011) Race, Ethnicity and Age. In Settersten, R. & Angel, J. (eds), *Handbook of Sociology of Aging*. New York, Springer, pp. 83–102.

Myles, J. (1984) *Old Age in the Welfare State: The Political Economy of Public Pensions*. University Press of Kansas, Lawrence.

National Association of Pension Funds (2011) *Workplace Pensions Survey*. NAPF, London.

National Audit Office (2012) *Regulating Defined Contribution Pension Schemes*. Report by the Comptroller and Auditor General. HC 466 Session 2012–13. NAO, London.

National Confidential Enquiry into Patient Outcome and Death (2010) *An Age Old Problem: A Review of the Care Received by Elderly Patients Undergoing Surgery*. NCEPOD, London.

Navarro, V. (1976) *Medicine Under Capitalism*. Praeger, New York.

Nazroo, J. (2006) Ethnicity and Old Age. In Vincent, J., Phillipson, C. & Downs, M. (eds), *The Future of Old Age*. Sage Books, London, pp. 62–73.

Neugarten, B.L. & Hagestad, G.O. (1976) Age and the Life Course. In Binstock, R.H. & Shanas, E. (eds), *Handbook of Aging and the Social Sciences*. Van Nostrand Reinhold Co., New York, pp. 35–55.

Newman, S. & Hatton-Yeo, A. (2008) Intergenerational Learning and the Contributions of Older People. *Ageing Horizons* 8, 31–39.

Newton, B., Hurstfield, J., Miller, L. & Bates, P. (2005) *Training a Mixed Age Workforce: Practical Tips and Guidance.* Department for Work and Pensions, London.

Newton, B., Hurstfield, J., Miller, L., Ackroyd, K. & Gifford, J. (2003) *Training Participation Amongst Unemployed and Inactive People.* Institute for Employment Studies, Brighton.

O'Connor, J. (1973) *The Fiscal Crisis of the State.* St Martin's, New York.

O'Rand, A.M. (2000) Risk, Rationality, and Modernity: Social Policy and the Aging Self. In Schaie, K.W. & Hendricks, J. (eds), *The Evolution of the Aging Self: The Societal Impact on the Aging Process.* Springer, New York, pp. 225–249.

Office for National Statistics (2008a) *Occupational Pensions Schemes Survey 2007.* ONS, London.

Office for National Statistics (2008b) *Pension Trends.* ONS, London.

Office for National Statistics (2008c) *Prescriptions Dispensed in the Community: Statistics for 1997 to 2007: England.* ONS, London.

Office for National Statistics (2011a) *Older People's Day 2011.* ONS, London.

Office for National Statistics (2011b) *Trends in Life Expectancy by the National Statistics Socio-Economic Classification 1982–2006.* ONS, London.

Office for National Statistics (2011c) *Pension Trends: Chapter 8: Pension Contributions.* ONS, London.

Office for National Statistics (2011d) *Pension Trends: Chapter 6: Private Pensions.* ONS, London.

Office for National Statistics (2012a) *Population Ageing in the United Kingdom, its Constituent Countries and the European Union.* ONS, London.

Office for National Statistics (2012b) *2011 Census – Population and Household Estimates for England and Wales, March 2011.* ONS, London.

Office for National Statistics (2012c) *Pension Trends: Chapter 4: The Labour Market and Retirement.* ONS. London.

Office for National Statistics (2012d) *Pension Trends: Chapter 7: Private Pension Membership.* ONS, London.

Office of Fair Trading (1997) *Inquiry into Pensions.* OFT, London.

Ogg, J. (2005) *Heatwave: Implications of the 2003 Heat Wave for the Social Care of Older People.* Young Foundation, London.

Organisation for Economic Co-operation and Development (2006) *Live Longer, Work Longer.* OECD, Paris.

Ottaway, S. (2004) *The Decline of Life: Old Age in Eighteenth Century England.* Cambridge University Press, Cambridge.

Pahl, R. (2000) *On Friendship.* Polity, Cambridge.

Pahl, R. & Spencer, L. (1997) Friends and Neighbours. *New Statesman*, 26 September, pp. 36–7.

Parker, R. (1990) Elderly People and Community Care: The Policy Background. In Sinclair, I., Parker, R., Leat, D. & Williams, J. (eds), *The Kaleidoscope of Care*. HMSO, London, pp. 5–22.

Parliamentary and Health Service Ombudsman (2011) *Care and Compassion? Report of the Health Service Ombudsmen on Ten Investigations into NHS Care of Older People*. TSO, London.

Parsons, T. (1942) Age and Sex in the Social Structure of the United States. *American Sociological Review* 7, 604–16.

Parsons, T. (1943) The Kinship System of the Contemporary United States. *American Anthropologist* 45, 22–38.

Parsons, T. (1951) *The Social System*. Collier-Macmillan, London.

Passuth, P. & Bengtson, V. (1996) Sociological Theories of Aging: Current Perspectives and Future Directions. In Quadagno, J. & Street, D. (eds), *Ageing for the Twenty-First Century*. St Martin's Press, New York, pp. 12–30.

Pemberton, H., Thane, P. & Whiteside, N. (2006) Introduction. In Pemberton, H., Thane, P. & Whiteside, N. (eds), *Britain's Pensions Crisis*. Oxford University Press, Oxford, pp. 1–27.

Pensions Commission (2004) *Pensions: Challenges and Choices. The First Report of the Pensions Commission*. The Stationery Office, London.

Peston, R. (2008) *Who Runs Britain?* Hodder, London.

Phillipson, C. (1981) Pre-Retirement Education: The British and American Experience. *Ageing and Society* 1, 392–414.

Phillipson, C. (1982) *Capitalism and the Construction of Old Age*. Macmillan, London.

Phillipson, C. (1993) The Sociology of Retirement. In Bond, J., Coleman, P. & Peace, S. (eds), *Ageing in Society*. Sage Books, London, pp. 180–199.

Phillipson, C. (1998) *Reconstructing Old Age*. Sage Books, London.

Phillipson, C. (2002) *Transitions from Work to Retirement: Developing a New Social Contract*. Policy Press, Bristol.

Phillipson, C. & Ogg, J. (2010) *Active Ageing and Universities: Engaging Older Learners*. Universities UK, London.

Phillipson, C. & Smith, C. (2005) *Extending Working Life: A Review of the Research Literature*. Department for Work and Pensions, London.

Phillipson, C., Ahmed, N. & Latimer, J. (2003) *Women in Transition: A Study of the Experiences of Bangladeshi Women Living in Tower Hamlets*. Policy Press, Bristol.

Phillipson, C., Bernard, M., Phillips, J. & Ogg, J. (2000) *The Family and Community Life of Older People*. Routledge, London.

Phillipson, C., Leach, R., Money, A.-M. & Biggs, S. (2008) Social and Cultural Constructions of Ageing: The Case of the Baby Boomers. *Sociological Research Online* 13(5). At http://www.socresonline.org.uk/13/3/5.html. Accessed 12 September 2012.

Pillemer, K., Wells, N.M., Wagenet, L. et al. (2010) Environmental Sustainability in an Aging Society: A Research Agenda. *Journal of Aging and Health 23, 433–453*.

Pitt-Watson, D. & Mann, H. (2012) *Seeing Through British Pensions: How to Increase Cost Transparency in UK Pension Schemes*. Royal Society of Arts, London.

Polivka, L. (2000) Postmodern Aging and the Loss of Meaning. *Journal of Aging and Identity 5, 3–14*.

Pollak, O. (1948) *Social Adjustment in Old Age*. Social Science Research Council, New York.

Pollard, E., Bates, P., Hunt, W. & Bellis, A. (2008) *University is Not Just for Older People: Working Adults Perceptions of and Orientation to Higher Education*. Department of Innovation, Universities and Skills, London.

Portes, A. (1998) Social Capital: Its Origins and Application in Modern Sociology. *Annual Review of Sociology* 24, 1–24.

Powell, J. & Chamberlain, J. (2012) *Social Welfare, Aging and Theory*. Lexington Books, Lanham.

Powell, J. & Cook, I. (2007) *New Perspectives on China and Aging*. Nova Press, New York.

Putnam, R. (2000) *Bowling Alone*. Simon Schuster, New York.

Ray, M. & Phillips, J. (2012) *Social Work With Old People*. Palgrave Macmillan, London.

Riley, M.W. (1987) The Significance of Age in Sociology. *American Sociological Review* 52, 1–14.

Riley, M.W, & Riley, J.W., Jr (1993) Connections: Kin and Cohort. In Bengtson, V.L. & Achenbaum, W.A. (eds), *The Changing Contract Across Generations*. Aldine de Gruyter, New York, pp, 169–190.

Riley, M.W. & Riley, J.W., Jr (1994) Structural Lag. In Riley, M.W., Kahn, R.L. & Foner, A. (eds), *Age and Structural Lag: Society's Failure to Provide Meaningful Opportunities in Work, Family, and Leisure*. Wiley, New York, pp. 15–36.

Riley, M.W., Johnson, M. & Foner, A. (1972) *Aging and Society*. Vol. 3: *A Sociology of Stratification*. Russell Sage, New York.

Riley, M.W., Kahn, R.L. & Foner, A. (eds) (1994) *Age and Structural Lag: Society's Failure to Provide Meaningful Opportunities in Work, Family, and Leisure*. Wiley, New York.

Robb, B. (1967) *Sans Everything: A Case to Answer*. Nelson, London.

Roberts, N. (1970) *Our Future Selves*. Allen & Unwin, London.

Rowe, J.W. & Kahn, R.L. (1998) *Successful Aging.* Pantheon, London.

Royal College of Psychiatrists (2011) *Report of the National Audit of Dementia Care in General Hospitals 2011.* RCP, London.

Royal Commission on Population (1949) *Report.* HMSO, London.

Sass, S. (1989) Pension Bargaining: The Heyday of US Collectively Bargained Pension Arrangements. In Johnson, P., Conrad, C. & Thomson, D. (eds), *Workers versus Pensioners: Intergenerational Justice in an Ageing World.* Manchester University Press, Manchester, pp. 92–112.

Schaie, K.W. & Achenbaum, W.A. (eds) (1993) *Societal Impact on Aging: Historical Perspectives.* Springer, New York.

Scharf, T., Phillipson, C., Kingston, P. & Smith, A. (2002) *Growing Older in Socially Deprived Areas.* Help the Aged, London.

Schiller, N.G., Basch, L. & Blanc-Szanton, C. (1992) *Towards a Transnational Perspective on Migration, Class, Ethnicity and Nationalism.* New York Academy of Sciences, New York.

Schuller, T. (1989) Work-ending: Employment and Ambiguity in Later Life. In Bytheway, B., Keil, T., Allat, P. & Bryman, A. (eds), *Becoming and Being Old.* Sage Books, London., pp. 41–54.

Schuller, T. & Watson, D. (2009) *Learning Through Life: Inquiry into the Future of Lifelong Learning.* NIACE, Leicester.

Sennett, R. (1998) *The Corrosion of Character.* W.W. Norton, New York.

Sennett, R. (2006) *The Culture of the New Capitalism.* Yale University Press, New Haven.

Sennett, R. (2012) *The Rituals and Pleasures of Co-Operation.* Allen Lane, London.

Serra, V., Watson, J., Sinclair, D. & Kneale, D. (2011) *Living Beyond 100.* International Longevity Centre–UK, London.

Settersten, R. (1999) *Lives in Time and Place: The Problems and Promises of Developmental Science.* Baywood Publishing Company, Amityville, NY.

Settersten, R. & Angel, J. (2011) Trends in the Sociology of Aging: Thirty Year Observations. In Settersten, R. & Angel, J. (eds), *Handbook of Sociology of Aging.* Springer, New York, pp. 3–16.

Settersten, R. & Angel, J. (eds) (2011) *Handbook of Sociology of Aging.* Springer, New York.

Settersten, R. & Trauten, M. (2009) The New Terrain of Old Age: Hallmarks, Freedoms, and Risks. In Bengtson, V., Gans, D., Putney, N. & Silverstein, M. (eds), *Handbook of Theories of Aging,* 2nd edn. Springer, New York. pp. 455–470.

Sewell, W.A. (1992) A Theory of Structure: Duality, Agency and Transformation. *American Journal of Sociology* 98, 1–29.

Shanas, E. (1979) The Family as a Social Support System in Old Age. *Gerontologist* 19, 169–174.

Shaw, J. (1971) *On Our Conscience.* Penguin, London.

Sheldon, J.H. (1948) *The Social Medicine of Old Age.* Nuffield Foundation, London.

Shilling, C. (2008) *Changing Bodies: Habit, Crisis and Creativity.* Sage Books, London.

Smeaton, D. & McKay, S. (2003) *Working After State Pension Age: Quantitative Analysis Research Report 182.* Department for Work and Pensions, London.

Stack, C. (1974) *Strategies for Survival in a Black Community.* New York: Harper.

Stearns, P. (1975) *Lives of Labour: Working in a Maturing Industrial Society.* Croom Helm, London.

Stearns, P. (1977) *Old Age in European Society: The Case of France.* Croom Helm, London.

Steinig, S. & Butts, D. (2010) Generations Going Green: Intergenerational Programs Connecting Young and Old to Improve Our Environment. *Generations* 33, 64–69.

Taylor, P. & Urwin, P. (2001) Age and Participation in Vocational Education and Training, *Work, Employment and Society* 15, 763–779.

Tett, G. (2010) *Fool's Gold.* Abacus, London.

Thane, P. (1978) The Muddled History of Retiring at 60 or 65. *New Society*, 3 August, 234–6.

Thane, P. (2000) *Old Age in English History.* Oxford University Press, Oxford.

Thomas, K. (1974) *Religion and the Decline of Magic.* Peregrine Books, London.

Thomas, K. (1976) Age and Authority in Early Modern England. *Proceedings of the British Academy* LX11, 205–248.

Thompson, P. (1999) The Role of Grandparents When Parents Part or Die: Some Reflections on the Mythical Decline of the Extended Family. *Ageing & Society* 19, 471–503.

Thomson, D. (1989) The Welfare State and Generational Conflict: Winners versus Losers. In Johnson, P., Conrad, C. & Thomson, D. (eds), *Workers versus Pensioners: Intergenerational Justice in an Ageing World.* Manchester University Press, Manchester pp. 33–56.

Tibbitts, C. (ed.) (1960) *Handbook of Social Gerontology.* University of Chicago Press, Chicago.

Timmins, N. (2008) 'Paupers' Warning Over Private Pensions. *Financial Times*, 30 May.

Titmuss, R. & Titmuss, K. (1942) *Parents Revolt: A Study of the Declining Birth Rate in Acquisitive Societies.* Methuen, London.

Townsend, P. (1957) *The Family Life of Old People*. Routledge & Kegan Paul, London.

Townsend, P. (1962) *The Last Refuge*. Routledge & Kegan Paul, London.

Townsend, P. (1981) The Structured Dependency of the Elderly: The Creation of Policy in the Twentieth Century. *Ageing and Society* 1, 5–28.

Townsend, P. (1986) Ageism and Social Policy. In Phillipson, C. & Walker, A. (eds), *Ageing and Social Policy*. Gower, Aldershot, pp. 15–44.

Townsend, P. (2007) Using Human Rights to Defeat Ageism: Dealing with Policy-induced 'Structured Dependency'. In Bernard, M. & Scharf, T. (eds), *Critical Perspectives on Ageing Societies*. Policy Press, Bristol, pp. 27–44.

Townsend, P. & Wedderburn, D. (1965) *The Aged in the Welfare State*. Bell, London.

Treas, J. & Marcum, C. (2011) Diversity and Family Relations in Aging Society. In Settersten, R. & Angel, J. (eds), *Handbook of Sociology of Aging*. Springer, New York, pp. 131–144.

Troyanksy, D. (1989) *Old Age in the Old Regime*. Cornell University Press, Ithaca.

Tsang, P. (2009) Age and Performance Measures of Knowledge-Based Work. In Czaja, S. & Sharit, J. (eds), *Aging and Work: Issues and Implications in a Changing Landscape*. John Hopkins University Press, Baltimore.

Turner, B. (2008) *The Body and Society*. 3rd edn. Sage Books, London.

Twigg, J, (2000) *Bathing: The Body and Community Care*. Routledge, London.

Twigg, J. (2006) *The Body in Health and Social Care*. Palgrave Macmillan, London.

Uhlenberg, P. & De Jong Gierveld, J. (2004) Age Segregation in Later Life: An Examination of Personal Networks. *Ageing & Society* 24, 5–28.

United Nations (2009) *World Population Ageing 2009*. UN.

Universities UK (2010) *Patterns of Higher Education Institutions in the UK*. UUK, London.

Urwin, P. (2004) *Age Matters: A Review of Existing Survey Evidence*. Employment Relations Research Series 24. Department of Trade and Industry, London.

Vickerstaff, S. & Cox, J. (2005) Retirement and Risk: The Individualisation of Retirement Experiences? *The Sociological Review* 53, 77–95.

Vickerstaff, S., Phillipson, C. & Wilkie, R. (eds) (2011) *Work, Health and Well-being: The Challenges of Managing Health at Work*. Policy Press, Bristol.

Victor, C. (2010) The Demography of Aging. In Dannefer, D. & Phillipson, C. (eds), *The Sage Handbook of Social Gerontology*. Sage Books, London, pp. 75–95.

Victor, C.R., Scrambler, S.J., Bond, J. & Bowling, A. (2004) Loneliness in Later Life. In Walker, A. & Hennessey, C. (eds), *Growing Older: Quality of Life in Old Age*. Open University Press, Maidenhead, pp. 107–126.

Vincent, J. (2003) *Old Age*. Routledge, London.

Von Kondratowitz, H.-J (2009) The Road to Moralization of Old Age. In Edmonson, R. & Von Kondratowitz, H.-J. (eds), *Valuing Older People: A Humanist Approach to Ageing*. Policy Press, Bristol, pp. 107–122.

Vullnetari, J. & King, R. (2008) Does Your Granny Eat Grass? On Mass Migration, Care Drain and the Fate of Older People in Rural Albania. *Global Networks* 8, 139–171.

Walker, A. (1980) The Social Creation of Dependency in Old Age. *Journal of Social Policy* 9, 45–75.

Walker, A. (1991) Thatcherism and the New Politics of Old Age. In Myles, J. & Quadagno, J. (eds), *States, Labor Markets and the Future of Old Age Policy*. Temple University Press, Philadelphia, pp. 19–35.

Walker, A. (1996) Intergenerational Relations and the Provision of Welfare. In Walker, A. (ed.), *The New Generational Contract: Intergenerational Relations, Old Age and Welfare*. UCL Press, London, pp. 10–37.

Walker, A. & Foster, L. (2006) Ageing and Social Class. In Vincent, J., Phillipson, C. & Downs, M. (eds), *The Futures of Old Age*. Sage Books, London, pp. 44–53.

Walker, A., Gordon, D., Levitas, R., Phillimore, P., Phillipson, C., Salomon, M. & Yeates, P. (2010) *The Peter Townsend Reader*. Policy Press, Bristol.

Warnes, A.M., Freidrich, K., Kellaher, L. & Torres, S. (2004) The Diversity and Welfare of Older Migrants in Europe. *Ageing and Society* 24, 307–326.

Weber, M. (1905/1930) *The Protestant Ethic and the Spirit of Capitalism*. Unwin and Hyman, London.

Weiss, R. & Bass, S. (2002) *Challenges of the Third Age: Meaning and Purpose in Later Life*. Oxford University Press, Oxford.

Wellman, B. (1998) The Network Community. In Wellman, B. (ed.), *Networks in the Global Village*. Westview, Boulder, CA, pp. 1–48.

Wellman, B. & Wortley, S. (1990) Different Strokes from Different Folks: Community Ties and Social Support. *American Journal of Sociology* 96, 558–88.

Whiteside, N. (2006) Occupational Pensions and the Search for Security. In Pemberton, H., Thane, P. & Whiteside, N. (eds), *Britain's Pensions Crisis*. Oxford University Press, Oxford, pp. 125–140.

Willetts, D. (2010) *The Pinch*. Atlantic Books, London.

Wolff, E. (2007) The Adequacy of Retirement Resources Among the Soon-to-be-Retired, 1983–2001. In Papadimitriou, D. (ed.), *Government Spending on the Elderly*. Palgrave, London, pp. 315–342.

World Bank (1994) *Averting the Old Age Crisis*. Oxford University Press, Oxford.

World Health Organization (2001) *Active Ageing*. WHO, Geneva.

Wright, S. & Lund, D. (2010) Gray and Green? Stewardship and Sustainability in an Aging Society, *Journal of Aging Studies* 14, 229–249.

Yeates, N. (2001) *Globalization and Social Policy*. London: Sage.

Yi, Z. & George, L. (2010) Population Ageing and Old-Age Insurance in China. In Dannefer, D. & Phillipson, C. (eds), *The Sage Handbook of Social Gerontology*. Sage Books, London, pp. 420–429.

Young, J. (1999) *The Exclusive Society*. Sage Publications, London.

Zaidi, A. (2006) *Pension Policy in EU25 and its Possible Impact on Elderly Poverty*. European Centre of Social Welfare Policy and Research, Vienna.

Index